A
FAITH MISSION
PILGRIM

REV. JOHN D. HAMILTON
1927 - 2007

Published by
Maurice Wylie Media
143 Northumberland Street
Belfast
Northern Ireland
BT13 2JF (UK)

Publishers' statement: *Throughout this book the love for our God is such that whenever we refer to Him we honour with Capitals. On the other hand, when referring to the devil, we refuse to acknowledge him with any honour to the point of violating grammatical rule and withholding capitalisation.*

For more information visit
www.MauriceWylieMedia.com

CONTENTS

FOREWORD

I first met John Hamilton in 1986, when I had only just come back to God after 10 years of what I would call 'heavy backsliding'. I was sitting in a house meeting near Ballymena and am not sure whether it was out of nerves (I was never in a house meeting before) but as John was ministering, every time he would look at me, I would smile like a Cheshire cat (smiling from one ear to the other). And sometimes, when that look would come, I would be bold enough to say, "Amen" or suchlike.

John had something flowing through him that I had never witnessed before… it was the love of God. Because of this love… fear within me drove me out of that house once the meeting ended; for I could not handle the pure love that he carried.

Before I got out through the door, a hand grasped my arm, it was John. He said, "Before you go home tonight, come back in and see me." I responded, "Yes!" but, in truth, I had no intention of going back in. When I went outside I quickly got into the car, and told the others who were with me to get in, but would they get into the car? No! I wish I could tell you here, they didn't get in because of their love for me, but no, the reason they did not get into the car was because they were being nosey. They wanted to know why John wanted to see me. I tried my best to persuade them to get into the car but to no avail. I had no choice but to go back into that house and see what this man wanted.

When I went back in through the doorway, he looked over and saw me; he then took me into a private room and started to minister to me. It was all new to me. This hard guy me, who was not scared of the gross darkness of life, all of sudden had tears running down my face, uncontrollable: I was scared of love.

What took place in that room[1] was like Jacob in the Bible, never being the same again. I will go into this later.

Shortly after that time, I would become like an adopted son to him, and we would travel together, spend time together and I had the honour of ministering with him up to near the time of his death.

I learnt many things from my spiritual father, some of which I will share later with you, from funny to tear-jerkers.

What I can say? I would never have known God the way I do today except for the likes of Rev. John Hamilton. Like the young Faith Mission Pilgrims who went before him set an example, John would become my example. I pray, as you read this book, that I have done honour to the one I can honestly say, *'whose shoes I am not worthy to unfasten.'*

Maurice Wylie

---

1   More details of this experience in 'A Bride Prepared for the Master' published by Maurice Wylie Media

CHAPTER 1

WITH OR WITHOUT

The words of John Hamilton:

I don't think I will ever forget the first time I gave my testimony. It was in a small mission hall with about 40 people present. I was only maybe a month or so converted, and a young man from Edinburgh had taken me to a little place called Elphinstone, to a Faith Mission Conference.

It was all new to me, everything about the experience was all new to me. The conference had two speakers. After the first speaker had spoken, there was a break for tea, and then the second speaker came on. What was going to take place next, I would never forget the rest of my life.

On the platform there was a table nicely spread with lovely crockery and nice cake-stands and everything was just so well presented: and that was for those who had the privilege of sitting on the platform, those special people.

But it was different for us poor people sitting in the stalls. When it came to tea-time, I saw two ladies come out of the kitchen, one carrying the biggest kettle I ever saw in my life. The other lady carried a big zinc basin full of cups, but these were special cups for the poor people, each one had a crack in it or a chip taken out of it. Then after those two came another with the bags of buns, and that was your afternoon tea. The lady with the kettle moved the kettle to me and said, "With or without?" Well, I found out when poured, it wouldn't make any difference the 'with or without' as it was stewed to glory!

The time came when the young man who brought me to the conference went up onto the platform and spoke through the microphone, saying, "There's a young fellow here tonight, he's not been long saved; would you like to hear his testimony?" And of course, they said, "Yes, get him up": fresh blood. When I look back I don't think they had had fresh blood for years in that conference. He went on to say, "You'll be glad to know I've brought my young brother with me this evening." I thought, 'I cannot remember seeing your young brother.' Then he said, "He has only been saved for a few months." And I thought, 'This is marvellous.'

Then he said, "He used to be a barman!" I thought, 'This is unbelievable. That's what I was!' Next: "Would you like to hear his testimony?" Sitting in the front row I said, "Yes, bring him on, I would love to hear his testimony!" You see, I was thinking, 'I'll listen to what he says, and if ever I'm asked to give my testimony, I'll just say what he says, because his life was like mine, this would be a good starting point for me to learn how to give my testimony. But the place went silent and nobody moved.

Then he announced again for his brother to come forward. I thought 'what is keeping his brother? He's either an old age pensioner, or he's finding it difficult to walk; must be something wrong with him.' My problem was I couldn't turn my head to see if anyone was coming to the front. My mother always said, "Never look back: it's bad manners." And you know, even at 25 years old, I still was keeping that rule, after years of getting slapped on the back of the head if I had turned around. But I sure was tempted as I thought 'Who is this guy's brother, as I knew his family?'

Then it was if the whole floor opened up as I heard words coming from the platform and the guy's finger pointing at me, his finger looked like 12 feet long… "It's you, my brother!" I said back to him, "Me?" (pointing my own finger to my chest).

My mouth fell open. I don't even remember rising off my seat, or walking to where they were three steps up to the platform; as I lifted my foot to go to the first step, I fell up the first two, and on the third one, I ended up grabbing the table cloth. Everything that was on the main table, the cups (don't forget: these were the non-chipped cups!), plates, buns, were now making a racket as they were falling all to the ground. Can I ask, have you ever given your testimony standing on sugar? It will be the sweetest testimony you will ever give!

The whole place was in chaos. When the people all stopped laughing, and after the great build-up of announcing me to come forward, I said… "Well, friends, I'm glad I'm saved." And I turned and went and sat down on the front row again. Needless to say, I was never asked back there again.

Anyway, I can't stand people who do not tell the truth, and when I got outside I said to the fellow who brought me, pointing the finger at him, "Don't you be going around telling everybody you're my brother, because you're not!" He responded, "But you are my brother!" I said, "Look, I've only got two brothers, and you're definitely not one of them." It was then he started to tell me of this great family of God, that I now belong to: that he was my brother and I was his.

Are you part of this family of God? If not, you can be! It is only through the blood of Jesus, only through that saving knowledge of Christ, that I can say to you, I'm so glad that I belong to the family of God. I have so many brothers and sisters now, it's unbelievable.

I wish to share with you how I ever got to be from a barman not wanting to know God, to a servant of the Most High ministering the power of the Holy Spirit. Are you ready?

CHAPTER 2

COUNTING BALDHEADS

It was a wee place in Coatbridge, just on the outskirts of Glasgow, in Scotland that I was born. There were six of us; boy, girl, boy, girl, boy, girl – how's that for an order of service! I was raised in what I thought was a normal home, but maybe for you, it was abnormal. My mother was a Roman Catholic, and my father a Protestant. Every Sunday there would be the same argument in our home. Like, there were arguments through the week, but Sunday just brought with it that more heated exchange. My mother would say (speaking of the children), "They're going to the Catholic church today!" And my father would say, "Oh no, they're going to the Protestant church today!" Catholic church, Protestant church, you know what happened? We got sent to both, how about that for punishment? Each Sunday we had four services to attend and four more through the week. And when we argued the point of not going to both of them, the same statement was released… "And you'll go there until you are 16!" Now if you a mathematician, you just count that up; Sunday was my most enduring day of the week. I just did not enjoy it going through all those services. I think the only Sunday I enjoyed was the prize-giving service. For perfect Sunday attendance, the whole Hamilton family received Bibles and multiply that over the sentence we had received until we would be 16, that would be a lot of Bibles that would end in our home. I want you to note something: it was perfect attendance, not perfect behaviour!

Every year at prize-Sunday the minister would announce, "John Hamilton for perfect attendance at church, a lovely copy of the Word of God." And I would say under my breath, "Aw, not another Bible." You see for perfect attendance you received a Bible, but for good attendance you received a book. After each presentation when we would return home, my mother would say, "Let me see your Bibles... right, put them in the cupboard." If the underground church had known about the Hamilton's, they would have been able to have a supply of Bibles each year!

Anyhow, this year Toshie (a friend of mine) was sitting beside me at the prize-giving and I could not believe what he was saying to me. He said... "I wish I could get a Bible." I thought, 'this guy is bananas.' I said to him in case I was hearing things, "You really want a Bible?" He said, "Aye! But I'll not get one." I said, "I have good news for you, this is your lucky day, you are going to get a Bible." Right under the minister's nose I was arranging movement of goods, I would give Toshie my Bible and for once, I would receive a book.

I could not wait till my name got called and off I went to receive my Bible for perfect attendance. Coming back to the seat I waited and waited, eagerly waiting on Toshie's name to be called. Then the announcement came... "For good attendance Toshie come forward to receive 'The Dandy Annual.' I nearly jumped out of my seat, I was so excited. The agreement would be that on Monday at school,

Toshie would bring the Dandy Annual and I would bring my Bible and we would swap. Oh, I could not wait: my perfect plan was in place. I had outwitted my mother, as I knew she would ask when we went home, 'let me see your Bibles; now put them in the cupboard.' So, my plan was I would wait unto the next day, then smuggle my Bible out of our home and swap it for the Dandy Annual.

I never slept that Sunday night, and up early for school and for the first time during my school terms I ran to school, with my Bible stuffed up my jumper, so no-one could see it. There was Toshie waiting for me at the school gate with the Dandy Annual. I cannot remember what I was taught that day in school, because sat on my knee under the school table lay open my first ever Dandy Annual. My study that day was on Keyhole Kate and Desperate Dan – my best day at school!

When I got home from school, my Aunt Mary had called in, she was in the Brethren Church, and my mum and she were having tea. Just to impress my Aunt, my mother said, "Let your Aunt Mary see that lovely Bible you got yesterday!" I don't know if it was a brainwave or a brainstorm, but I thought, 'I'll just give her last years' Bible – she'll never know the difference. They all look the same.' So, I took last year's Bible and I gave it to her. Anyway... everything was going so well until she put her glasses on. She looked at the inscription and said, "Oh, they've made a mistake." By that time, I was running halfway down the hall, my mother shouting, "What mistake? come you here, John!" My mother, looking at the inscription, said "That is no mistake! What did you do with your Bible you got yesterday from church?" And with trembling lips I told her I swapped it for the Dandy Annual, emphasising

'Annual' (thinking I got a good bargain). It did not matter: a real good thumping I got in front of my Aunt.

The reason I am sharing this story is: every Sunday I attended 4 services, every year I received a Bible for perfect attendance; and yet I did not know why Jesus came. In fact, I had no idea. The only God I seem to be aware of was an angry God, a God who judged people, a God who was always ready to condemn them. I never once heard of the love of God. I never once heard that Jesus came to die for my sins. Now I don't blame the church that I attended in that sense, because when the minister stood up, he never changed his introduction in all the years I had been attending. Each Sunday morning, "My text for today is…" and it was time for me to switch off.

Now I know you likely have never switched off in church, it's likely the person sitting near you in church does that. But I was an expert in pretending to enjoy something and all the time my mind would have been somewhere else. If I was sitting on the balcony I would count all the ladies' hats. If he was still was not finished, I then started to count the bald heads. For the bored, there's always something to count!

CHAPTER 3

HALF-PINT HAMMY

I could not handle all the in-house fighting with my mum and dad. Because of that, I ran away to Glasgow before I reached 16 years old. But when I got there, I discovered two things. One, I didn't have a job; two, I had nowhere to sleep. And that surely was a bad start to my new adventure in life. I found a newspaper and scrolled through it looking for work and found a column, 'Situations Vacant' and there I saw a job that would fit me.

When I tell people that know me what I read, most of them laugh. It read, 'Smart young man, must have good appearance.' But it was not that, which caught my eye. What caught my eye was three words… 'Must live in!' The job that was being advertised was a trainee barman in the biggest hotel in Edinburgh. And so, I went for an interview.

Standing there in the cocktail bar the manager asked me many questions, and I told him many lies just to get the job. Then he said, "Stand up!" I said, "I am standing!" "You're what? You're too wee for the job, laddie. You'll never reach the pumps! Away you go and try them," he said. I went over and tried them, even going standing on my toes but could not reach them. He said, "I'm sorry, son, you're no good to me if you can't reach the pumps." I was so disappointed, not because I was losing out on the job; I was losing out on the room. That's all I wanted, the room!

As I began to walk out of the bar, my eye caught an empty beer crate in the corner and I said to him, "Excuse me." He answered, "What is it?" I said, "If I can take the crate over to the pumps then I can reach them!" He said, "The job is yours!"

It was then that I was christened in the bar 'Half-pint Hammy' (how about that for a name?); and I got the room. And when I walked into the room, I could not believe it: there was only one bed, and only one barman (that was me) in that bed. Because being raised at home, there was six of us in one bed, three at the top, three at the bottom. You went into bed alive and came out dead! Boy, how I enjoyed a whole bed to myself!

CHAPTER 4

WHEN DOORS OPEN

I used to think that people who went to church were the ones who were going to Heaven and yet why are they so miserable - hello? And the people in the pubs were all going to Hell. So, what I was about to experience rocked my boat. At the appointed time the bar doors swung open and the customers came in and they were joyful, happy, excited, enjoying each other's company, could not wait to buy each other a drink… the opposite of what I saw in the church; (minus the drink – but you know what I mean).

I remember standing at the bar that day thinking 'I don't want to go to Hell but I want to be happy, so I'll join this lot.' Now God gives us free will, isn't that right? After-all, God says, *'I have set before you life and death, blessing and cursing' therefore choose life, that both you and your descendants may live'* (Deuteronomy 30:19). Did you read that? God said to 'choose': that means you have freedom to choose, otherwise He would have made us into robots without a will. And He also gives us a clue to which one He wishes us to pick… *'therefore choose life!'* God's will for His people is life!

That day I decided that the church and Christians were not for me. These people in the bar would be my people and I was going to have a good time and, most of all, I would be happy! I would do what they do, I would live as they live and try and wipe away my childhood unhappiness. Yes, my childhood unhappiness; can any child be as unhappy as I was?

I was born what was called a 'sickly child', always being sick. My parents were told not to expect me to live. The parents' doctor was a great doctor and to help my parents out, and to give me a better chance to live, he offered to adopt me and take me abroad. This would enhance my chances of living. My mother would not give me up: what was hers, was hers. The doctor then advised one last suggestion. She would take me out in the early mornings, when the air would be its purest. She took me with her in the mornings when she would be scrubbing the floors to support the family.

I was the weakest one of my brothers and sisters and being the smallest didn't help either. But I was always sickly and had no life, the last to get food, the one who received the hand-me-down clothes that had holes in them and of course, it was no longer the style. And let me tell you something: even at that young age, I would try suicide three times.

I didn't talk about it, I tried it. That's how "happy" I was. I was tired of wearing a mask whether at church, with my friends, just in life. That mask is on many faces. It's the mask that says, 'ha, ha, ha,' and inside people are broken and crying. Some are so broken they can never be made whole except through the power of God. And God knows your every need. He knows where you are, and He knows how you are.

With all this unhappiness, my mother concluded it was part of what was making me sick and she took me to a psychiatrist, one after another. I knew I wasn't crazy but I was searching, even to the point of spiritualism. I tried everything, but each ended the same: I was more frustrated. I became depressive, full of fear. Even if I was not alone, I felt lonely, full of insecurity. But in my company, you would never have guessed that was the real me. I would have received the academy award for being the best actor of the year. I had a specific face for the public to see, and that face deceived many people. You could hear me laughing the loudest, you could hear me joking the most; but inside I was weeping. I can't remember a night I did not weep before I fell asleep. But never once did I call upon God. Never once did I go to church. And the reason for this; I never saw happy people in church. Church was like a graveyard… full of dead people. The sadness is, young people are watching, they are taking it all in and if someone spoke to me in church, it was, "Shh! Boy, you're in church, behave!" I wanted so much for someone to reach me, but the only God I knew of was that God in Heaven, away up there, while I am down here, and He was always ready to strike me if I walked out of place.

CHAPTER 5

THE DAWN OF HOPE

Walking along the Prom on Portobello Beach on the 28th August 1952... I will never forget it. Gathered on the beach was up to 300 people and they were singing the hymn which I found out later is called 'Blessed assurance, Jesus is mine!' The noise of the waves, the music and the words touched my heart as I heard...

> 'This is my story, this is my song,
> Praising my Saviour all the day long.'

I never saw such happy people! I thought, 'They can't be Christians – they're too happy!' And I thought, 'Maybe it's an American group that has come over, a new religion has arrived in Scotland!' That's what I thought!

On the makeshift platform was a sign: Faith Mission Campaign. On the platform stood five young men. And I want to express what challenged me the most about these young men – their faces were radiant!

At that moment (and I am sure you never do this), but I actually ended up having a chat to myself. I remember saying to me, yes me! 'Look at them! They don't smoke, they don't drink, they don't gamble, they don't, don't, don't: and they are HAPPY! Look at you. You do all these things but you are miserable.' And that was a true assessment of my life. I was 25 and I had a drink problem, depression and my life was still in a mess. Here I was standing looking at these young men, and there was just something about those young men that arrested me. They were so fulfilled, clean and wholesome. I was the very opposite.

I had decided that before they started preaching I would take myself off, as I knew what would be coming next… 'My text is going to be…' was I in for a shock! I was taken completely off guard. The words he spoke were these: "I believe God is speaking to someone here tonight." Phew! That just blew my mind. He said it again, but this time he pointed his finger right across the Prom. And I remember that finger looking like six feet long as he said, "I believe God is speaking to someone here tonight and it is you!" Somewhere inside of me I could hear a shout, 'Yes! Of course, get on with it!' But he didn't wait on me answering, he continued… "If it's you, I want you to know: Jesus loves you!"

Three words that can change your life – Jesus loves you! Those words went right into my heart. Simple words that I had sung many times during Sunday school in the chorus, 'Jesus loves me, this I know.' But that night, something happened. That night I just knew that those three words were not just words, but they are eternal truths: Jesus loves you!

For the first time I began to cry in public. Oh, I had cried many times behind a closed door, but never in public, and trust me: in front of nearly 300 people. What a way to start! And worse still, I could not control my emotion; tears just flowed down my face. As I stood there I said to myself, 'You know what you need? You need Jesus. You need Jesus, I tell you, John Hamilton, you need Jesus!' That was a revelation to me.

I had no sooner said it, than one of the Faith Mission lads was standing right beside me, and he said, "Excuse me, sir." Immediately the mask came back on me and I said, "Get lost!" "Oh no," he said, "You're the one that is lost!" Now, friend, is that not some answer? 'You're the one that is lost'! He continued, "Jesus came to seek and to save the lost."

There was something about this young man that really bugged me and I wanted rid of him; I just wanted to see the back of him walking away from me because I didn't like the challenge. I didn't like the way that he was not speaking vague or general about this God, he was speaking as if he knew God personally, as if Jesus was beside him. And it frightened me, but then it hit me: I was frightened of love.

You know; we need more people like those young men who don't preach about a God in heaven, but know about the God who walks with them, the God of love.

'How could I get rid of him' I thought. I had the answer, I would pour a lot of filth into him, and he'll start running the whole way to his church, crying like a baby, but how wrong I was. The more filth I poured on him, the more he stood there and said,

"John, that's not what it's all about. It's about Jesus and His love for you!"

I thought, 'If he says that again, I'll thump him.' Because every time he said it, I felt a lump in my throat. And then he said to me, "Would you like to come on Friday night to the closing meeting in the Baptist church?"

I thought, 'Here's my chance now. If I say No, he'll keep standing and if I say Yes, he will leave.' So, I answered, "I would love to come."

Now, humanly speaking, I could not be there, because I had to work, especially Friday nights. So, I asked, "What time do you need me to be there for, and who's the speaker?" Oh, I thought I was ever so clever. He handed me his card and looked me straight in the face and said, "Are you sure you will come?" I said, "Look, if I say I'll come, I will be coming." Looking me eyeball to eyeball he said, "God bless you, we'll be praying for you." No one had ever said that to me, no one had cared enough! But that young fellow, a total stranger, committed himself to me. We need Christians like that.

It was six months later that I found out that night those young lads stayed up all night prayed for my salvation, aye me, John Hamilton. How about that, Christian? Who are you praying and sacrificing your quality time for?

During that week in my sleep all I could hear was, 'God is speaking to you. You need Jesus. Jesus loves you' and so on. And on Thursday night, it was worse, like a battle was going on inside of me. I thought, 'I wish it was morning'. These Bible-punchers has got me at a sentimental time. 'I'll be alright in the morning. I'll be back to my old miserable self.' Imagine wanting to return to your old miserable self?

Can I ask you, "Do you believe that God answers prayer? Do you?"

In the morning as soon as I arrived behind the bar the manager called me over saying, "I want to speak with you." What is it?" I said. "I want you to change your day." I thought "These Faith Mission boys have phoned him up and said, 'Give that wee barman a day off today!'"

"Eh, when – when do you want me to change it to?" "Today," he replied. I thought, 'He can change it from any day but Friday, as this is the day of the meeting I have been asked to.' "Well, Vera has a wedding on Friday, she's asked, can you change with her?" And I could not believe it: my mouth answered, "I'll change!" Everything I thought that would have kept me away from the meeting was now being taken away in front of my eyes. But I still had a trick up my sleeve.

Instead of going to the meeting that night, I decided to go to the dance. Right in the middle of the dance floor I was dancing with this beautiful girl and out of nowhere this irresistible desire to get to the Baptist Church was so strong that I said to the girl, "Excuse me darlin', I've got a date somewhere else." And I walked away and I left her on her tod. And I won't tell you what came out of her mouth as I walked away!

Now this Baptist Church was not the easiest place to find in Portobello. It is not a normal church building, but an upstairs hall. I looked for Baptists and I couldn't find them. I found every church in the area but the one I'm looking for, some were even padlocked. And in that moment, I became angry. As anger rose up in me, I said to myself: 'Hmm, every pub is open and every church is closed. I'll forget about this and go and have a drink.'

I looked at my watch and my watch had stopped. So, I looked at the town clock to see what time it was, and it wasn't the clock that got my attention, it was what was underneath the clock. A sign said, 'Baptist Church'. Isn't that wonderful? You might call it coincidence. I call it God-incidence. I call it God answering prayer.

I looked both ways: no, I was not practising how to cross the road, I was checking to see if any of my mates would see me going into a church, and I was one hour late! How about that for your first time back to church? I went up stairs and opened the door, and the man at the door looked at me, and he said, "I think you've come to the wrong place." I asked, "Is this not the Baptist Church?" "Yes." he answered. I answered, "Well, I have come to the right place." And he looked at me again, "No" he answered, as he x-rayed me. You see: I was a teddy-boy!

One of the young men who was on the beach was on the stage preaching and suddenly he stopped, directing his voice to the back, "Oh, John Hamilton!" And of course everyone looked round to the back of the hall, to see who was John Hamilton. I think they thought the Bishop had arrived, instead was this five-feet nothing trying to get into church. Do you remember the Teddy Boy style? The jacket had false shoulders, the haircut and the tie, and those great big crepe-soled shoes. I wish they would bring them back again, it would make me 3 or 4 inches taller.

The young man shouted again, "Come on in, John!" and wouldn't you know it, the only seat that was vacant was on the front row of the hall, right in front of where the young man was. I'm not sure if it was because he stopped in the middle of the preaching, or shouting out my name, or them seeing this small person that looked like a Teddy Boy; but the place was in utter silence until… I took my first step and squeak, squeak, squeak, squeak. I could feel the daggers looking at me, sorry the eyes of the lovely congregation. They were all suited up; and here was I, so looking out of place. I sat right at the front waiting, knowing all eyes were fixed on me.

The young man switched from preaching to giving his testimony and everything that young fellow said was my life in duplicate. And there came a cry in my heart that night: 'If only you were like me, if only you had this peace, if only you had this joy…' He said, "Tonight you can have it."

I nearly fell off my seat: I couldn't believe it. He said, "We're going to bow our heads, we're going to close our eyes. I'm going to ask you tonight if you want Jesus Christ to come into your life and be your Saviour. If you just raise your hand I will see it, I will pray for you, and you'll be born again." I said to myself, 'That's what I will do, I'll raise my hand…'

Do you know, I could not lift my hand? I did understand what was going on, but a spiritual battle was taking place for my life which I was not aware of. The sadness is that many Christians don't realise the spiritual battle that goes on. But I knew hell itself was fighting for my soul – I believed that. But remember what I told you: five men had prayed for me.

The young man went on… "Maybe you're unable to raise your hand? If you would just look up, I'll see you." I tried to look up, but I couldn't, I could not even lift my head. It was as if a heavy hand was on top of my head. Then the young man said, "Perhaps you couldn't raise your hand, perhaps you couldn't look up? But if you just come and see me after the service, I'll have a word of prayer with you. I'll point you to Scriptures that will make you wise to salvation. You'll leave this church tonight knowing your sins are forgiven and you are a child of God."

I remember thinking, 'Yes, that's what I'll do. I'll see this Bible-puncher afterwards, and I'll pray, and I'll go out of here as a child of God.' That's what I really wanted to do. We sang the closing hymn, and closed with the benediction; the meeting was over. I got up out of my seat and ran, not to the front, but ran out through the door at the back.

The battle was still raging for my soul as, somehow, I wanted to be 'caught' but I was now on the run. But guess what? The young fellow got up and he ran after me! And worse still, he outran me. Catching up with me, he said, "Stop!" You're not leaving here until you get yourself right with God." Oh, I tell you folks, we need such men for this day that we live in. Jesus said, 'I will make you fishers of men' (Matthew 4:19). This young lad was just doing that… finding fish that was trying to escape the net – and I was short in size but a big fish, seeking in reality to be caught by a God that loved people.

I responded to him by saying, "Look, I'm sorry for the way I spoke with you!" He said, "Forget about it!" This in itself shocked me, as Christians I knew give up so easily on people, this fellow was stuck to me like glue. He continued, "God is speaking to you, John." I said, "Look, I can never be a Christian." He asked me, "Why?" I answered, "I am such a sinner. You don't know the people I run around with. I'm just no good, I never have been any good, I never will be any good. I'm just a sinner." Painting myself as black as I could, I thought he'd say, 'Jesus is wonderful, but He's not that wonderful.'

I continued, "Also, I could never keep it up. Even if I did try I would fail. I'm the weakest of the weak, and I know what I'm like, and I wouldn't like to make a fool of this Jesus. I just don't want to do it and then in two or three days' time, be back to the old John Hamilton again." He responded by, "John, I tell you this. If you give your life to Jesus Christ, He'll not only save you, He'll keep you. You can be kept by the power of God." This guy was not giving up and the fear that caused me not to put my hand up, not to look up, to run out of the hall, was rising again within me, I could nearly taste it. I said to him, "Look, just leave me."

When you pray all night for a person, God will give you the wisdom to reach that person, the right words to speak to them. God will show you when to be still, when to go on, when to speak, when to be silent. Try it! Try a whole night praying for a person, and the next time you meet them, you won't make a mess in reaching them. At that moment I knew if he took another step of pushing me I would walk away, walk away forever. But God had given him the ability to sense where I was in being caught in God; and he said, "All right, John, I'll leave you in the hands of God." Now listen reader, what does the Bible say? *'It is a fearful thing to fall into the hands of the living God.'* (Hebrews 10:31)

He went over to the bookstall and lifted a book, reaching it to me, he said, "I'd like you to read it." "Oh, I said how much is it?" He said, "I'm giving it to you." Now that really touched me. A total stranger was giving me this book, and all he asked me to do was read it.

CHAPTER 6

FREE AT LAST

You see how wise that young man was? He gave me a book of testimonies. I think there were 25 testimonies from people in all walks of life: they came to the Cross; they all came to a point in life where they decided to follow Jesus Christ. I went home that night, and I read that book from cover to cover, and I wept the whole way through it. It was at 2 a.m. in the morning that I got down on my knees beside my bed. I wasn't caring, I was not caring what anybody would think or say, or what anybody would do. I just knew that I knew, at that moment I had to give my life to Jesus Christ.

When I got down on my knees, I discovered a terrible truth. I didn't know how to pray, I had no clue. All my life I had rejected God, and now in my moment of need, how do I call upon Him, how was I to do it? How was I to come? What was I to say? I was now wondering what to do, when I was prompted to open the book of testimonies again, and it fell open at the testimony of a drunkard. At the end of his testimony there was a prayer. It was the only prayer that was recorded in the book.

'Jesus, be merciful to me a sinner,
and come into my heart,
and be my Saviour.'
Amen.

I can tell you that with my whole heart I prayed that prayer. I cried
out to God for mercy. I cried out to God for salvation. I don't
know how long I spent on my knees, but I knew when I got up I
was a child of God. My sins, which were many, were all forgiven.
I felt so clean. I felt good. Never did I believe that such peace and
joy could be mine as it was in that moment. Never did I think that
Jesus could be so real and so near to me. I felt He was so near that
if I had put my hand out I could have touched Him.

What a transformation! I knew I was now a child of God. I knew
that I would never be the same again from that moment. Isn't that
wonderful? I knew my old life was over; a new life had begun. I
did not fully understand it, but I sure did enjoy the experience
of it. I knew that I had entered into a new dimension of life that
I'd never touched before. And it was wonderful. Jesus became a
living, bright reality to me. I wanted the world to hear: He lives!
I want the world to know: He saves! He heals! Listen to me: not
only in that moment was I saved, I was healed of many hurts,
many wounds, many scars. I was totally set free from my drink
problem, from all depression. It was not a part-redemption, it was
full redemption. From the crown of my head to the soles of my
feet, Jesus had made me whole. From bondage into liberty. Out
of darkness into His glorious light. I also felt as if chains fell off
my body: the hand of God was placed onto my life.

It was 9 a.m. and I ran down the stairs and said to the manager, "I'm leaving this place now!" He said, "Why?" My response, "I'm a Christian now!" He looked at me and said, "Yea, sober up!" Shocked, I responded by saying, "I have never been as sober in all of my life. I'm telling you, I'm a Christian now!"

He said, "I don't believe you. You're the biggest rogue that ever worked in this bar. You steal and you lie!" Well, that was true. I said, "That has all changed." He then asked, "When did you become a Christian?" I said, "2 a.m. this morning." He said, "There's no churches open at 2 a.m. in the mornings, I know you're lying now! How would you become a Christian if you weren't at church?"

I said, "I started to say this prayer… 'Jesus, be merciful to me a sinner, and come into my heart, and be my Saviour, Amen'… and <u>he</u> started to cry!

"Hey," I said, "do you want to be a Christian?" He said, "I am a Christian, I go to church every Sunday." I thought, 'if am a rogue, you're a bigger rogue!' But I said, "Well, I don't know about that, but I know I'm a Christian." He said, "We need to test you." Wondering what he was meaning, I said, "What do you mean, test me?" He said, "You'll work for one more week, and we'll find out if you're true or false. Okay?"

I was going to say, 'No, no way will I work here one more week,' when I remembered the words of the young evangelist. He had said, "Jesus not only saves you, but He keeps you. You will be kept by the power of God!"

Let me tell you something: in those few hours I planted my feet firmly on the Word of God. Not my feelings, not my intellect, but the Word of God. And based on that, I said Yes to working another week; and what a week it was...

I would not like to go through it again, but I have news for you: I did go through it! And you know why? Because God's Word cannot be broken. Isn't that something! What God says, He does. What God promises, He gives. And *'God is not a man, that He should lie'* (Numbers 23:19). And I was kept, and am still being kept to this day, all those years ago.

From the first day of that week, the folks would have come in taunting me with every unimaginable thing one could think of. "He's gone hallelujah, and joined the hallelujah brigade."

First words were normally, "You're a Christian!" I would say, "That's right, I'm a Christian." They even brought in a huge Bible and planted it on top of the bar and said, "So, you believe in this?" "Of course I do, of course I believe it." (Even though I could not quote a verse from it.)

But let me tell you this, and this hurt me deeply. That morning I had to go to the local Christian bookshop and buy a Bible. Yet, my mother's cupboard was full with Bibles. For a Scotsman, that is a hard thing!

They began to tear the pages out of the big Bible and roar statements at me, "John (my name) the Baptist, it's full of prostitutes and homosexuals – it's pornography! And you believe all of this?" I said, "Yes!" They said, "Well, if you believe in all of this, then turn this water into wine!" With the first evening shift over, I went upstairs to my bedroom and said, "O God, I'll never make it. I'll never make it. They're too much for me. I don't have the answers. Too much for me, Lord."

Right there in that little room, God spoke these words..."Son, I'll never leave you, and I'll never forsake you. I'll never, never let go of your hand." (Deuteronomy 31:6)

Had it been audible, it could not have been stronger. As a matter of fact, I initially thought it was an audible voice. I looked round the room, and there was no-one to be seen. And when I discovered that God spoke to His people, it's in the Bible, then I realised it was God that spoke into my spirit that night. I fell to my knees and said, "O God, if You will never leave me, I will never leave You. I need You more than You need me."

I want to tell you something... He has NEVER broken that promise, through thick and thin, through many deep waters, through many sorrows, through many trials and many tribulations: my God has proved true to His Word. '*When you pass through the waters, I will be with you; and through the rivers, they shall not overflow you. When you walk through the fire, you shall not be burned, nor shall the flame scorch you*' (Isaiah 43:2). What a God we have! What a relationship that is ours, that we are one with God the Father, God the Son, and God the Holy Spirit. Oh, that the world would know that Jesus lives, that Jesus saves, that Jesus heals, that Jesus delivers! The world needs to know and yet, sadly, even some in the church don't know. Do you know who God is? I went through that week not just somehow but triumphantly! It was God who brought me through.

Throughout Edinburgh, it spread like wildfire: 'Half-pint has gone hallelujah!' And the pub crowd all came to see the great sight – what a sight it was! – wee me. I had purchased a great big Thompson Chain Reference Bible, and I didn't even know where Genesis was. And they had said, "Aw, come on, we'll give you a week." Wasn't that generous of them? It's been a long week, all those years ago: I hope they're not holding their breath.

Every time they saw me, it was, "It's the Half-pint who's gone hallelujah"; until one day, they started to say, "You're the real hallelujah, then!" Now, wasn't that a testimony of our Lord's saving grace!

The Church Language: my first meetings I attended... was I in for a shock, especially the way they talked. Do you know the church has its own language? Everything was new to me as I sat there in the meeting soaking in as much as I could about this Saviour who saved a sinner like me.

As normal, one of the men would go up to the front and share their testimony. As he was sharing, he told of his brother out in the field. My, my I thought... why was he out in the field? Was he a farmer? Then he said, his brother had been out in the field for three years. Gosh, this guy is in trouble, I thought. Then he said, "he wants to stay out in the field longer!" Before I realised, I stood up and shouted, "for goodness sake... will someone bring him in!"

Then the personal one happened after a meeting...

He asked "How long do you spend in the closet?" I said, "What?" The man looked at me and repeated, "John, how long do you spend in the closet?" I thought and said to him, "Do you not think that is very personal?" He said, "I am trying to gauge you for ministry." I think my eyes rolled around in my head, I did not understand why he needed to know how long I spent in the toilet, so my answer was… "As long as it takes!" He said, "Brother, that is the right answer: you need to stay in the closet until you have a breakthrough!" I walked away thinking, "I stay in the closet as long as I have toilet roll!"

CHAPTER 7

THE FIRST CONVERT

My best friend Stewart was in hospital, and I went to see him in the Royal Infirmary in Edinburgh. I wanted to tell him what Jesus done in my life, and I told him what I told you, but maybe not in as much detail. His wife was sitting beside his bed as I told him, and I could see steam rising out of her nostrils, till it was nearly coming out of her ears. She was getting angrier and angrier, until she could not contain herself.

She burst in with "You! You're no good, you're just no good, and you'll never change. A leopard will never change its spots, and that's what you are. You've just been no good for my husband. You're just no good!" 'What venom,' I thought. In the middle of the torrent of abuse I said, "Agnes, that is all changed." But, I could not convince her. You see, there are some people who you will not convince.

But, I had come to see my friend, who had never been in church in his life, and he was lying there in that bed and he said, "John, don't laugh when I tell you this. All my life John, yes, all my life, I wanted to be a Christian." I said to him, "You can be a Christian now!" The flamethrower interrupted by saying, "Don't be so silly! How can my husband get out of bed and go to church?" I said, "He doesn't have to get out of bed to go to church."

With tears in his eyes he said, "John, what do I have to do?" I responded, "Stewart, all you have to do is pray." Agnes interrupted again, "You're not going to be praying here, are you?" I looked her right in the eye and said, "You've just said, that he cannot get out of bed; where else can he pray?" "That's it, if you're going to pray, I'm going out", and she went to leave. Stewart said, "I want to pray!" She said, "I'm away!"

Before I realised it, I shouted from the top of my voice, "Praise the Lord!" She likely thought that I was saying "Praise the Lord" because she had left, but in actual fact, it was because my best pal was going to pray the sinner's prayer. I got on my knees beside his bed and I said, "Stewart, pray this prayer."

The ward all fell silent as I started to pray, nurses stopped moving around and stood in respect, it was like time stood still for us, as they heard two men saying, "Lord Jesus, be merciful to me a sinner, and come into my heart and be my Saviour." I could feel Stewart's tears roll off the back of my hand. When we ended praying, I said to him, "How do you feel now?" He said, "I feel as if I have been washed in a washing machine, I feel so clean! I feel so good!"

I said, "You're a Christian now, you've joined the club of heaven. When you get out of that bed, you and I will evangelise Edinburgh!" Small ambitions, would you not say?

I looked at him and said, "See you next week!" My best pal was my first convert. My feet hardly touched the ground, I was so excited! We would be two soul winners!

I my feet hit the ground coming As my feet hit out of the ward. Agnes was standing and flames were still to be seen. Her first words out of her mouth were, "I suppose Stewart is a Christian now? Oh, you make me so sick." She continued, "I suppose you think you're the new Billy Graham?" I replied, "I'm not the new Billy Graham, but I'm telling you, don't take my word for it, go and ask him yourself, and he'll tell you!" She answered, "We'll see" and off she walked into the ward. But she was in for a shock as she walked through the ward to the last bed, where Stewart lay. He never told her; he never spoke; he never told her that he asked Jesus into his heart. Do you know why? Stewart was gone, he had passed away.

Dear reader, the story is in one sense sad, but yet also wonderful. Wonderful and amazing that my friend missed the train to hell and took the glory train to heaven. Let me remind you, he never been to church in his life, never heard a sermon, never heard a prayer… until that day: the day he accepted Jesus into his heart.

How many times have you heard the gospel? How many services have you attended? How many people have you prayed for? Are you actually saved? In that split moment, where will we spend eternity?

As I was leaving the hospital that day, God placed a truth in me: do you want to know what it is? God showed me, 'Tomorrow does not belong to man, only today.' Did you read that? 'Tomorrow does not belong to man, only today.' 2 Corinthians 6: 2 states, 'For

He says: in an acceptable time I have heard you, and in the day of salvation I have helped you. Behold NOW is the accepted time; behold, now is the day of salvation.'

I learnt that day that I would continue with that urgency, 'Oh God, wherever I am and wherever I go, let this be my testimony, that today is the accepted time for all men. And let me not be ashamed to tell it, because for some tomorrow could be too late.'

Today Jesus can be your Saviour. Tomorrow, He might be your Judge. *'Choose yourselves this day whom you will serve..., But as for me and my house, we will serve the Lord.'* (Joshua 24:15)

CHAPTER 8

LOVING THE AUTHOR

In those very early days of my new-found faith, it seemed there was born in me a tremendous hunger for the Word of God. I just loved the Bible, the book that I detested as a wee boy in Sunday School: the book that was given to me every year for perfect attendance.

I started to read from the beginning of the Bible, the Book of Genesis, and I ploughed my way through it, because I loved the Author of the book. I loved Jesus with this passion that it was almost agony. And it seemed that this hymn was a reality in my life…

> Heaven above is softer blue,
> Earth around is sweeter green;
> Something lives in every hue
> Christ-less eyes have never seen.
> Birds with gladder songs o'erflow,
> Flowers with deeper beauties shine,
> Since I know, as now I know
> I am His and He is mine.

When I look back over the years, what a tremendous relationship with Jesus I had... and am not just talking about attending church... can you say the same? Every day, brother, there were new revelations of God's love to me, and new manifestations of His power. There is nothing like the presence of the Lord. And everywhere I would go, I would tell them about the love of Jesus.

CHAPTER 9

FINDING A SPIRITUAL HOME

I don't believe God wants us to be spiritual tramps or nomads. If you have ever visited Edinburgh, you will know it has a church at the end of nearly every street. So, I started to go to the one nearest to me and began to work my way round them all. Some of them scared me, some left me cold, and in some I thought, 'I will never get out alive'. But within me was this rising desire 'to belong.' I wanted to belong to a family of God. I wanted not only to belong to a place where I could not only receive, but give, support.

I remember one Sunday morning not going out to church, I was tired trying to find a church. And I just prayed; "Father, please show me, please show me where You would have me worship and serve You." Did you ever ask where God wanted you to be? That evening I went out at 6 p.m., really believing that God would show me in that hour the very place where I should be part off. And suddenly I ran into old Anne. She was 70 years young, she'd just got saved about 4 years earlier, and I tell you, that woman was on fire. You came near her and you got singed. There she was standing with a great handful of gospel tracts. She said, "Excuse me sir, would you like a gospel tract?"

"I would love one!" At this she nearly fell off the footpath with shock, because I took one; then with that extra boldness she said, "We're having a service tonight. Would you like to come into it?" When I said, "I would be delighted," I nearly had to use smelling salts to bring her to her senses.

Later that night as I walked through the entrance of that church, I knew I had found my home. Isn't it a marvellous thing to know you have found your home? Home is not about perfection, it's about you being allowed to be you in Christ. When I scanned around it looked like a motley crew had gathered. Their singing would not win Oscars, but their fellowship and love for each other, I would never forget. I listened to a blind minister, a Mr Robertson from the Congregational Church. Oh, he knew the Word of God. He stood like 10 feet tall and thundered the gospel. And of course, anyone behind me received nothing, because I drank it all in. I was just so thirsty for God!

The church would hold all-night prayer meetings, fasting, street evangelism, door-to-door visitation. I was never in a church like it, so active and hungry for the things of God. So, my church walk started with running, not slothful, not half-hearted, or cold, but hot… running into the things and ways of God. Tell me: are you running?

With the church fellowship, outreaches, spiritual exercises of fasting, seeing God move, it developed in me a greater hunger to know God. It was a wonderful time and I thought I had everything and God had me.

CHAPTER 10

A LITTLE BIT OF RELIGION

My friend in the church was Gordon. He and I were doing a lot of door-to-door outreach. But one day I saw Gordon coming walking to me and I knew something different had taken place with him. I said, "Gordon, what's happened to you?" He said, "It's the baptism." I said, "What? It's done that for you, the baptism? I'll see the minister next Sunday, and I'll get baptised." I thought he was speaking about water baptism; I thought, 'My goodness, if water baptism has done that for you, it's time I got baptised in water.' Gordon quickly interrupted, "John, it's not that kind of baptism." You see, I was so ignorant still of the Bible. I said, "What kind is it then?" He said, "It's the baptism of the Holy Spirit. All you have to do is pray!"

I was so eager to have everything God has for me. My attitude was Jesus paid the full price, not a half price. Therefore, why do we settle of half-cup measures of God, when there is a fulness of God to be attained?

I grabbed him by the sleeve and said, "Come on then, let's pray!" "Oh," he responded, "We can't pray in Princes Street, we need to go into a church." "So, let's find a church then," I urged.

It was 11.30 p.m. at night, and I still remember it so well. We entered the side door of the church building and went in. Getting down onto our knees, we started to pray. People always complained that Gordon and I were too loud in our praying. Even in prayer meetings, someone would nudge him or me in the ribs and say, "There's no need to be shouting when you pray, God is not deaf!" We always would have answered, "He's not nervous either." Suddenly as Gordon was praying in this old vestry of a church, he came out with a beautiful tongue.

Well, being truthful, at that time fear came upon me again, I was petrified. I thought, 'this guy has gone bananas, what the heck has happened to him now?' So I went over to him and shocked him. "Gordon, what on earth is going on with you?" Note I didn't say, "What is right with you?" I said, "What's wrong with you?"

And as I was shaking him, I remember looking at his face and it was shining, as if a flashlamp was shining through him. I said to God, "I want that... but I don't want this!" You see, I didn't understand; and what we don't understand, most of the time we condemn. In the middle of me shaking him, he said, "What's wrong?" I said, "You tell me; what's all this gibberish?"

He didn't respond by saying, "It's tongues," or "It's in the Bible." He just said, "That's the baptism." I said, "If that's the baptism, well, no thank you. I don't want that baptism." All he said was, "John, don't let the devil get in." Quickly I responded, "You're too late. The devil is in with both feet!"

I was about 12 months saved at the time, and I was about to experience real spiritual warfare, or whatever you would like to call it. Suddenly, it seemed that there were two powers at work in my life now. When that young man said, "Don't let the devil in.' I tell you, right from that moment I turned fully to Jesus. I wanted to be a fighter for God. I didn't want to be mealy-mouthed and weak-kneed and spineless. I wanted Jesus to get the best out of my life. When he said, "Don't let the devil in." I asked, "Well, what do I do?" He said, "Just get back down on your knees again and start praying again!"

Of course, I got back down on my knees and I don't remember if Gordon prayed for me, or did he lay hands on me. All I know is that my hands shot up. And I cried out to God, "Oh God, baptise me in the Holy Spirit!" Suddenly, the heavens opened. And I want to describe what took place.

Now some that may read the following will find it hard to accept God can be so real but let me ask… 'have you really read your Bible or you just a listener? One who listens to what the preacher says and nothing more, nothing less?' Yet the Bible says, *'Study to show thyself approved unto God.'* (2nd Timothy 2:15). *'For when for the time you ought to be teachers, you have need that one teach you again; which be the first principles of the oracles of God; and are become such as that need of milk, and not of strong meat.'* Hebrews 5:12

The Holy Spirit entered the room in a mighty power, so mighty and so powerful that I was thrown bodily right across the room, not once but many times. And I tell you, that little room became a spiritual battlefield. Not one part of my body was hurt or damaged in anyway. Times I was laughing, times I was crying, hard to describe, but at the same time. My face was soaked with tears and all I wanted to say was, "Jesus, I love you!" And out of my inner being this language came forth in tongues. Oh I tell you, I loved Jesus in that moment. It felt as if every ounce of me loved Him. Earthly words could never comprehend the love of the Father I felt at them moment of time. It was like electricity going all through my body and it was now shortly after mid-night.

We sat there all night in worship to God, it was 8 a.m. in the morning when we left the vestry and I still could not speak English. Every time I opened my mouth, tongues came out. And here was me on my way to work… Oh Lord: you have to help me!

It was extremely difficult at work that day. A lady asked me something and I just turned round to speak and tongues came out. She jumped about six feet in the air. Then she screamed, and the manager came round and said, "What's the matter, madam?" "Oh, it's not me, it's this young man," she said.

Manager looked at me and said, "John, what's wrong with you?" I tried to speak, I really tried to speak. I tried that hard, twisting my mouth, moving my tongue in all directions and still tongues came out. Manager said, "John, don't come near me. You go home, you're sick." I had my own feelings but I couldn't even say what I felt. He said, "Excuse me madam, he's just had a little bit of religion, but he'll be alright." He sent me home, and I spent that day at home praising the Lord – with full pay!

CHAPTER 11

TEST THE SPIRITS

I have shared how Gordon and I would pray out loud, but tonight was the church prayer meeting and could I wait to go... I was excited! In my thinking, I thought, 'The minister will be glad when he hears what happened to me.' The prayer meeting had just started when I arrived and some of the members were on their knees, waiting on God or praying. My thinking was, 'I need to let the minister know what has taken place in me, but how do I do that?'

Combing the hall to see where the minister was, he was on his knees and a man was kneeling beside him. So, only way I could allow the minister to hear what God had done was gently squeeze myself between the man and the minister. I got myself squeezed between them, opened my mouth and a beautiful tongue came out. Immediately, the minister put his hand on my shoulder and nearly dislocated it.

He said, "You're not bringing that in here. That is of the devil." I said, "What? Of the devil. Then I don't want it!" He continued, "You're not splitting my church up." I never even thought of such, or would desire such for any church. What is happening?

I could not understand it. Now seems division was within the camp. I could feel it, and it hurt me, because I really loved these people. They were my brothers and sisters in Christ. You see I was experiencing God but I needed to back it with Scripture, but I was still a babe in Christ. The thing was... how could I deny what had taken place? Have you ever denied what God has done in your life because of a collar or someone who is a spiritual hairdresser? (Cuts the Word of God to suit their style!)

As the minister was pouring all types of wrath over me, that I was now of the devil. One of the deacons stood up and said, "Just a minute, Mr Robertson. What does the Bible say?" The minister said, "The Bible, says, *Test the spirits, whether they are of God.*" (1 John 4:1). The deacon said, "Why don't you just do that then. How can you say something is of the devil and you have not tried it against Bible ways of discerning?" The minister looked at me and said, "John, are you prepared for this?"

"Well," I said, "truthfully I don't understand it, but I'm prepared for anything that will prove not to you only but to me what I have is from God. And believe me, if it's not from God, then I don't want it either." We then all got on our knees again.

I forgot about all the people that were in the room, and I was away again into pure praise and worship of my God. A new dimension of praise and worship had broken out in my spirit. And it was glorious. Then the time came when the deacon and the minister placed their hands on my shoulders. This time the minister was gentler. Mr Robertson now spoke in this authority saying, "Tell me, brother, is Jesus Christ coming back in the flesh, or is He coming back in the spirit?"

Without a moment's hesitation I said, "Oh, praise God, He's coming back in the flesh." And the deacon who had stood by me, right there and then was baptised in the Holy Spirit, singing in tongues, not a hand laid on him, not a prayer offered. The minister said, "Pray for me that I might receive." I said, "I can't pray for you, you're my minister!" He said, "I command you to pray for me," and I said "Oh-h-h…" And nothing happened!

Well, something did happen. He said this, and I want you to note it. "There are some here tonight, and like me you have denied the power of God. Well, tonight, I cannot deny it. God has baptised John and our deacon in the Holy Spirit. But you will not bring this Holy Spirit into this church." Did you read that? "You will not bring the Holy Spirit into this church?" Can you have church without the Holy Spirit? It would seem the answer to that is yes, but it's man's church, not God's Church.

Rightly or wrongly, I submitted to his request, as he was my minister. After that night the deacon, Gordon and I would gather to pray and allow the '*gift* of the Spirit' to flow through us.

CHAPTER 12

DISCERNING THE DOOR

Then one night while the three of us were meeting, Gordon gave this word: he called it a prophecy; I really did not know what it was. But he said, "You will go to England. Doors will open for you, and a work will open for you there. From there, God will take you into new places, and you will bring Pentecost to that people."

Let me share something here... just because God says "Go!" does not mean it is immediate. Prophecy is confirmation of direction, and then God opens the door. But what does John Hamilton do? Because I did not understand that, I thought God needed a hand and that I would help Him. How we need people to help guide us into God's fulness for our lives!

I left my job, I left my home, and I travelled down to England. Guess what happened when I got there? Not one door opened, not one. I stayed there up to four months, could not get a job, nothing. Somehow, I sensed that my praying had dried up, there was a kind of struggle, a daily struggle: something had happened. God was trying to let me know I was in the wrong place. He was saying, "Go back!" But because my little band of Christians I had met was telling me to stay, of course I listened to them, thinking they would know more.

One morning as I was getting ready for breakfast, God spoke. I'll never forget it. He said two words... "Go home!" Listen carefully here, reader. When God Himself takes time out to speak directly to us, everything else must become a lesser priority at that moment. For when God speaks, direction is also in His voice. And how do we know we are His sheep? *'My sheep hear My voice, and I know them, and they follow Me!'* (John 10:27). How we, the Church, have watered down the Truth! It does not say, 'hear the voice of a minister', 'hear the voice of a teacher,' for that matter, 'hear the voice of John Hamilton.' The question is... are we hearing God's voice?

Oh, I did not care what the direction was when God spoke. I just knew one thing and one thing only. God had spoken; I was back in relationship with Him; I had heard His voice. I ran down the stairs and said, "I've just had a word from God." They said, "Oh, good, brother; and what did He say to you?" I said, "He just told me to go home." Their response: "That's not from God;" another one immediately said the same, "that's not from God." I said to them, "What do you mean, that's not from God?"

They said, "You know what is wrong with you?" "No, tell me?" I said. "Just because the way is tough and the doors are not opening as you want them to open, you're going to give in and go back home. You're not made of real stuff. There's an area of pride in you." I said, "All right, I'll stay!"

Friend, I knew that I knew when I said, 'I'll stay,' I had stepped out of the will of God for my life. I knew it 100 percent.

Just then the telephone rang. It was the manager from one of the jobs that I had applied for. He said, "You can start the job tomorrow." I said to him, what I had told him a few days earlier in the interview. "When I turned up today for the interview I did not realise that this would be a licensed grocer's; and I do not want to be serving drink." He reminded me that I would not be serving drink. He would put me on the bacon and cold meat counter. "Just say you will be there!"

I agreed that I would take the job. Coming off the phone I received the applause of the Christians, I got their smile of approval. But God's face... God hid His face from me.

CHAPTER 13

YOU'RE FIRED

Within six months I was back behind the bar again, pulling pints. I was back in the gutter, the things of God; the people of God no longer in my life. I will never even try and tell you what all took place in those two years of my life. But then there came a point in those two years when I would sell my soul to the devil. I became so full of hate and bitterness; I was ugly of soul. Even barmen were saying, "Jock, go and wash your mouth."

How could this man, meaning me, do that? Me, who cried out to God earlier, "Oh God, forgive me," in that little room and was forgiven, cleansed, every sin blotted out, every fetter broken, every bondage snapped? In the little vestry, the Holy Spirit had come upon me with so great a force my body did not hold up to it. A new tongue God gave me there. A place in Him I found, so much more; and yet, here was I at the other side of the bar. Let this part of my story be a warning for you! God requires of us obedience, whatever the cost, and whatever the smile or disapproval that men give you. God expects and demands, deserves our obedience. Outside of that obedience there is no safety for you; none.

For the next two years I stood right behind the bar serving drinks, in bad company, hanging out at all the other wrong places. I longed to escape the darkness that was surrounding me, I longed that much to escape it, that I tried suicide several more times.

But remember, God is faithful. *'As a Father pities His children, so the Lord pities those who fear Him.'* (Psalm 103:13)

What I did not know was that little Congregational Church was still praying for John Hamilton, now the backslider. They were fasting and praying for me. I can tell you this. Even in that dark season, I sensed prayers were being made for me.

During those bar years, no matter what the conversation was, how ugly it was, filthy and unclean, someone would bring up something about Jesus, and would refer to me by saying, "Did you not know Him?" An anger would rise in me, like Peter (Luke 22:54-62). I would deny I ever knew Him.

Then one day as I was serving behind the bar, I looked and behold, it was the blind minister who had arrived and sat down at the first seat in the place. The waiter went over to him to take his order. Do you know what his order was? Let me repeat, do you know what his order was? It was 'John Hamilton!'

The waiter came over to me, the closer he was getting to me, the more my mouth seem to fall open and time seemed to be slowing down. He said to me, "Jock, there's a vicar here wants to see you!" I pretended to look around the waiter to see who he was referring to. I said, "I don't know him!" He said, "Well, he knows you and he's asking for you – you'd better go and see what he wants."

I straightened my wee self-up, walking over trying to show I had it all going, putting my false face on I said, "Yes, what can I give you?" He may have been blind, but he was fearless. He grabbed me like there was no tomorrow and shouted with loud authority, "What is a child of God doing in this den of iniquity?" My face was in technicolour. I just pushed his hand away and said, "Who said I was a child of God? Do you want a drink or not?"

Was my heart hardened or not? I was hard. I had gone from reaching Edinburgh with the gospel to now, where the gospel couldn't reach me. Oh, if I could ever leave you anything here, reader, it's to keep your heart right before God at all times!

The minister responded, "I'm not leaving this place without you." I won't tell you how I responded; but I left him sitting.

You would not believe what happened shortly after that. I was serving customers and the owner came to me, not the manager, but the owner. He owned a string of pubs and called in every month to see how the trade was doing. This ungodly man came over to me behind the bar, stood right beside me and said, "John, I don't know anything about you, but if I were you, I would go with that man!" I said, "You're not me, and I've no intention of going with him."

Listen, God knows how to get our attention, and the next two words that came out of the owner's mouth, got mine – "YOU'RE FIRED!"

"I'm what? I said. He repeated, "You're fired!" I said to him, "You're one mug. You'll give me a month's money now, and I'll walk out of here, and I'll take my trade along with me." He said,

"Just you do that." I went upstairs and I packed my things and a few of his things, just for good measure. And boy, I can tell you when I was coming down those stairs, was I angry, yea, I was ripping mad, as we would say.

The owner gave me the month's wage and said, "Goodbye!" I never even answered him. I was so furious, I forgot about you know who sitting at the entrance, and yes, he was still sitting. He heard me coming with my belongings and he shouted, "Praise the Lord!" I said, "Look, Mr Robertson, when we leave this pub, when we get outside, you'll go your way and I'll go mine, okay?" "We'll see" he answered. I took him by the arm and led him outside.

He said, "John, listen. I want to hear no more of it. You're coming home with me, you're coming back to Scotland." I heard myself say, "Alright, I'll come." But this was only lip service.

Mr Robertson said, "Before we return home, a Christian family here has offered us boarding for tonight, we will be staying with them and then travel tomorrow to Scotland." When I walked into that home, the sight brought tears to my soul. They were all on their knees, praying for John Hamilton the backslider. They had never met me, they didn't know me, but here they were crying out to God to bring him home, back into His will.

But I was hard. I sat and smoked cigarette after cigarette, and they continued to pray as if I was not there.

Mr Robertson said to me, "Why don't you stop all of this fighting? Why don't you just surrender your life to Jesus again?" I said, "I want to come back. God knows I want to come back... but I feel nothing! Nothing! Nothing I feel, but guilt!"

He said, "John, take God at His Word. *'If we confess our sins, He is faithful and just to forgive us our sins and to cleanse us from all unrighteousness.'"* (1 John 1:9)

I knew it, I knew it. But the battle that raged inside of me was fierce. I turned to the minister and said, "Alright, I'll come." And he prayed for me, and then I prayed, the Christians that were gathered were in ecstasy... I felt nothing. But I knew, if I didn't come back then, I would never come back, the rest of my life.

CHAPTER 14

A LONG ROAD TO HOME

The next morning, my minister and I arrived back home in Scotland. I was back to church again, all night prayer meetings, street evangelism, door-to-door, etc. For six months I was doing everything that I done before; but one thing was missing and for me, it was a massive thing… the awareness that God was walking with me was now missing over my life.

When I witnessed, prayed, read my Bible, fasted, doing all the same as before, I never once felt God. God in that time never once allowed me to sense Him over my life. You see, I had become witness to a feeling in God rather than the Word of God settled. I hope you're taking in what I am sharing? God wants to wean His Church back to the Word of God, away from the gimmicks of men, away from the trivialities of churches, back to the unadulterated, pure Word of God. Are you taking heed? It's His Word that gives life, it's His Word that gives power, it's His Word that causes us to stand and not fall. Can you say, "Amen!"?

One night on the way to the prayer meeting with still no sense of His presence, when I entered the church hall the power of God fell again! I was knocked down to the ground by the power of God, and I lay prostrate on the floor. The people just looked on and the minister said, "We'd better leave John alone."

They all went out of the hall; I don't have a clue where they went that night. All I know was, I was before God… revelation after revelation poured into me. Oh, I can tell you that was so real that night, such an encounter with God! I knew, that I knew, God had a call over my life and I was to answer to it.

I went home in the early hours of the morning. By this time my parents were divorced. Now the first thing I had done when I got saved was to go back and find my mother and family. When I found them, I said, "I'm going to be the breadwinner. I'll look after you," and I did. This morning I returned back home and I told my mother, "God has called me." She was not a practicing Christian, and responded, "What do you mean, He's called you?" I said, "He wants me to go into Bible College. He wants me to be a missionary, an evangelist." She said, "How much is He going to pay you!" I said, "You're funny! You've got it all wrong! They're not going to pay me, I've got to pay them." She said, "And where are you going to get the money from?" I said, "God will provide!"

She was dumbfounded how a son would be so stupid… paying God! "Listen, mother, I'm telling you I'm going to Bible College. God has called me, I'm going. And as He provides my needs, I know He will provide your needs. Now don't be angry with me." She asked, "Do you mean you're going to walk out and just leave me? Do you not realise I will now have to go out and do more scrubbing?" (My mother scrubbed floors to bring in extra money.) When I look back over life, there is no easy way to follow Jesus.

I went back into my room and said, "Oh God, you've heard my mother's cry. Is this really Your call on my life?" And God, in His graciousness, spoke to me again the very word He had given to me that morning. I answered, "Whatever the cost, whatever it takes, I'll follow you." And I meant every word of it.

When I returned to my mother, she said, "Have you changed your mind?" I said, "No, mother, I haven't. I'm going." "Well," she said, "when you go out through that door, don't you ever come back. You're no son of mine. Do you know what the Bible says?" I asked, "What does the Bible say?" She replied, "Charity begins at home." (After all these years I still never could find that in the Bible that my mother quoted). I told her "God will look after both of us." She responded, "I don't believe you, I've got to work harder, and you're walking out on me. May God forgive you." Now reader, was that easy?

But what made it harder again: the church did not believe me either, that God had called me. Their response, "Your place is at home!" "You're going to spoil your testimony." "You cannot walk out and leave your mother." "Who do you think you are?"

Do you know what the church did? They had a special prayer meeting against the will of God for my life. All these years later, I know the only reason I am here is that God has kept me. They began to pray, "Lord, open John's eyes." "Open his ears!" "Bring him back into Your will again." There was me sitting beside them in the prayer meeting and all this was going around me. I ended up not attending any more.

I got accepted into the Faith Mission Bible College, with not a penny in my pocket. I need to tell you this… God provided every need to me, right down to the razorblade, that's our God.

One day, I felt prompted to go back and see my mother. I said to God, "The door is shut." God said, "I'll open it." The Bible College was in Edinburgh, so I just needed to take the bus. On my way to the bus, I met Mrs Murray, a real good supporter of the Mission. She said, "Hello, brother, where are you going?" I said, "I'm going home to see my mother." Immediately, my bus pulled up and as I went to get on it, she said, "God bless you, son," placing a bundle of tracts into my coat pocket. (She was known as the tract-giver.)

Have you noticed, ladies are experts for looking through windows and the person outside cannot see them watching? My mother was no different. She had seen me coming and locked the doors. I stood like a wee pup outside our home knocking the door, wondering what kind of welcome I would get. All I heard from the other side of the door… "What do you want?" It was my mother's voice. I said, "I want in!" Her voice came through the door: "I told you, you don't belong here!"

Oh, doesn't God have a sense of humour! He just drops a seed into your heart and you spring it out! I said, "If you don't want Mrs Quinn to hear what I've got to say to you, you better open that door." The door flung open, this large arm came at me at high speed, grabbed my coat and I was hurled into the hallway, with the door slammed shut.

Being sarcastic, she said, "Well, big boy! How are you doing?" I said, "You see me, overfed and underpaid." My mother spoke again: "Do you remember your words when you left here?" I asked, "What did I tell you?" She came back at me with: "Oh, have you forgotten them already?" I repeated, "You tell me: what did I say!"

"Oh, you told me that God would provide your need and God would provide my need, isn't that right?" I replied, "Yes mother, that's what I told you." She went to the dresser. Now take note to what she said to me. "Here's a bill that has come in. Where am I going to get £25 to pay that bill?" I said, "Let me see?" I put my hands into my pockets and rumbled around, pulling out the tracts that Mrs Murray gave me, and to my surprise, they weren't tracts, they were money notes, in fact £25 of them. I said to mother, "There it is."

She took off, bumping me out of the way (I am not hard to bump out of the way), into her bedroom. She'd had met a miracle and she couldn't come to terms with it. Within a few moments she called out to me, "Come you in here now." I ran in and saw my mother kneeling on the side of her bed, saying with a broken voice, "I want Jesus in my life." Oh, the joy I got from pointing my mother to the Lord! From that day on, she boasted to everybody, "Do you know Billy Graham? My son is just like him, my son's an evangelist!" Mothers! What can I say?

CHAPTER 15

HARNESSED AT LAST

After finishing Faith Mission Bible College, I was sent out with Tommy Shaw on our first outreach. I'm sure many of you will remember that Faith Mission would have used small caravans to host their teams, and Tommy and I were no different.

We were dropped off at this small caravan, given our directions for outreach, and told we're going to win the lost for Jesus; but then we found out, we couldn't even reach our stomachs: how on earth are we going to reach the lost? You see, when we opened the small cupboard, thinking it was full of food, it was empty. Not even the smell of food could be entertained.

Wee Tommy said, "Brother, what are we going to do?" I responded, "We're going to pray and ask God to send it." And I cried aloud. In fact, the both of us were crying, pleading to God; not sure if it was faith or hunger. But when we were finished praying, I said, "what about a wee cup of tea Tommy?" "Aye," he said. He went outside to fill the kettle with water. I heard a racket: he had tripped over a box of groceries that was set on the step. It had sausages, beans, Kit-Kats, everything, and I tell you, how we feasted! What had happened, I hear you ask? We were so busy crying out loud that we never heard the caravan door being knocked.

As I sat there eating, God rebuked me. He said, "You would cry for food because you are hungry. And outside, they are dying without the Bread of Life. Have you cried for them as loud?" Are you taking heed, Christian?

A few days later, there came a knock on the caravan door, and this lady was standing outside. We invited her in and asked who she was. She said, "I was just passing by and saw your Faith Mission Campaign." She told about her husband, who was lying seriously ill in hospital and she had been visiting him." She said, "I saw your banner and I thought, I must give this Mission something, I'll buy a box of groceries. We asked her, "What made you come with the groceries to us?" "She told, "As a wee girl, two Pilgrims came to our village, and I heard the gospel for the first time through them. It was then I gave my life to Jesus. And I would like to tell you that I have journeyed this life with Him."

It was during my first year in the Faith Mission I met my wife Zillah. We just knew that God had brought us together, and that we should marry. It was not long after that we married, and it would be until the day that one of us would depart this earth.

CHAPTER 16

A LOCAL PARISH

After seven years I left the Faith Mission and went into the United Free Church of Scotland as a minister in Gorebridge. When I took up the post, God promised me Revival for it. At the end of the first year, my deacons and the congregational board all came together and said, "It's no use, Mr Hamilton. The doors will close. There's no change here." Then one man said, "You know what is wrong? We're getting too much religion. We're getting too much of the gospel. We need to be more secular."

'Oh God,' I thought, not one of them had been hearing what I have been saying to them in the last year. I left that meeting walking up the steep hill on my way home, dragging my feet after me, energy zapped from me by counsel of the flesh. Zillah asked, "What's wrong with you?" I told her. She said, "What are you going to do about it?" I said, "Only one thing I can do? That's to get before the Lord!"

I called a special meeting, for those who hunger for God, who sought change in their life and the area, to come and pray. Every night we would meet to pray in our home. For six weeks we prayed every night, with not one night missing, not one night off. We cried to God for change; we read the Word; we had tea; then we would pray again. Some would leave our home in the morning and go straight to work, not having slept; such was their hunger for change.

One night when we just had finished a cuppa, we went back on our knees and started to pray. Suddenly, one of the men started to speak in tongues and no-one was near him. (He had never spoken in tongues before). I went to put my hand on him to say, "Don't be doing that!" Instead I heard myself saying, "You're being baptised in the Holy Spirit, Hallelujah!"

As I said that, a new tongue came through me, after all the years of it never happening. I called on the church committee to gather again and I said, "Instead of us going secular, we're going God. We're going to have a Faith Mission Campaign and God is going to move." Listen, reader: from that campaign, many that were saved went on to be missionaries, people in ministry today, just because of that campaign. God began to move, people were baptised in the Holy Spirit.

CHAPTER 17

ARE YOU SURE?

I have noticed over the years that many Christians have this mentality that their experience in God is that moment of being born again. Well, let me never take from that most important moment in any of our lives; but that was only the start of your journey in God. It was not your start and end combined.

Because we journey with God in this life, God said very clearly to me, "I want you to leave this church, and serve My Church." What a tremendous call! When I shared this with Zillah, again there was no argument. She said, "Then we must do it!" You must realise that the decision to leave the church was hard: we were leaving a salary and the house that came with the church job. In fact, we were making ourselves homeless.

When I told the deacons that I was leaving, they were asking, "Where are you going to?" I would say, "I don't know." You could see their gestures to each other, 'Oh, he's really gone over the top this time.' Then came the very reverend counsel... "Mr Hamilton, are you wise, walking out of this church with two children and a wife to support, and not knowing where you are going? Are you sure you're hearing from God?"

The amount of times I have heard from people, 'Are you sure you're hearing from God?'. My friend: firstly, God never gets it wrong. Secondly: learn to document and date it when God speaks to you, and if you can tick off 'yes', He has done what He has said to you; then you know for sure you are hearing from Him.

Imagine yourself as a parent phoning your 40-year-old, and after you say a few words, even a sentence, they say, "Who are you?" My, my, my, the church is so. When the Father speaks, we do not hear, because we do not know His voice (John 10:27-28).

Just as my notice was coming to an end, a surprise letter arrived in the post. Zillah's aunt had passed away, and she had left us her beautiful home in Pickering, Yorkshire, England, where we would live the rest of our days out. Within days, invite after invite started coming in. Not once did I need to advertise my ministry, not once had I prayed for God to open the door. Do you know why? Because I had walked through the door that He opened. When we do that, smaller doors open because He is the door that opens doors.

If you remember: all those years earlier when I heard about going to England, off I went, and everything crumbled around me. Now God had opened the door, He did not need John Hamilton, the arm of flesh to help. When He opens the door, no man can close it. (Rev. 3:8)

CHAPTER 18

THE SICK CHURCH

Why is it that, when it comes to Sunday morning, we seek to put on our false face and off to church we go. Consider this: when you look to your left and right next time you're in church, that person is going through something. They may not look like it, but they are. When you just go to give surface ministry, in other words, in and out of a church as a speaker, but not really getting involved with the people, you will notice that everyone likes you, everyone smiles, everyone talks to each other. But when you operate under the Holy Spirit, He shows you beyond the false face, beyond the nice clothes, beyond the big Bible you carry. And I was about to experience the beyond…

I was in Germany for ministry meetings and after each meeting people would queue for hours to chat with me in private, but this day would impact me. It seemed to me that every person, every Christian who came into that wee room, was in a dreadful state: one would be worse than the other; then when I thought it couldn't become worse, it did. The amount of sickness, uncleanness, bondages, divisions, and so on, that were in the lives of God's people, was unbelievable.

When I went to my bed that night, I could not shake off the heaviness that was upon me. I felt this dirt and uncleanness in my ears, on my hands. It was as if I had come out of a dirty bath full of dirt and it was trying to stick to me. I had never experienced such before this. You know what I thought? Here is God, who carries the burden of an unclean church, and me only in that room for a few hours, with a few people coming through, and how unclean I was feeling?

I cried out to God, "Oh God, can this be your Church? Can this be your people? So, weak, so unclean, so much in bondage and in fetters, so divided, one person against another, one family member against another, a house divided. Can this be the people your Son entrusted with the gospel?"

Out of that cry came this answer, "Tell My people that they have not yet fully realised the potential for God that lies within them." Note that, friend… Not to be given, not to be received in the future day: it's already there within you! Do you know the potential that is within you? The same Spirit that raised Christ from the dead dwells, lives, abides within your heart if you're born-again! (Romans 8:11). God is saying, "The very same Spirit that went right into hell itself and raised up Christ from the dead dwells within My people." Reader: you have to say, now that's potential! This is what the devil fears, you attaining the revelation of who you are in God.

This five-feet nothing that the Spirit of God lives and works through: I can't understand it, I cannot comprehend it. But I tell you: I live in the joy of Him. I live in the liberty of Him. I live in the strength of Him every day.

CHAPTER 19

THE CALL OF GOD CRAVES FOR...

"Tell My people that it is the potential that is within them. Tell them of the call of God that is upon them!"

Did you read that? The potential that's within you is only part of what God said. You also must know and understand the call of God over your life. *'As the Father has sent me, so .... I will send you!* (John 20:21)

Do not let that truth slide past you. Let it come into your being. "As the Father sent me.... So I will send you!" Put your name in there! "So I, being God, will send ... !"

What a calling over your life! God wants to empower you to send you! As the Father sent the Son under the anointing, He also wants to send you under the anointing... this is the will of God for your life! For the call of God craves for the potential in God!

The Father never gives part of Himself to us; He gave all of Himself in Jesus. Can I ask, what more can He give you? Beloved, there is no more, there are no more crosses that He will hang on, no more graves He will lie in, no more sin will He be cloaked in. He did it all for you! Learn to walk in the liberty of Christ, in His calling over your life. You do not need to apologise, no need for you to be weak or to say, "I cannot." Remember, *'I can do ALL THINGS THROUGH CHRIST JESUS!'* (Philippians 4:13). Not some: ALL!

CHAPTER 20

THE HANDS OF CHRIST

Out of those words, "Tell My people that it is the potential that is within them. Tell them of the call of God that is upon them" there came a beautiful vision… of His hands. They were held out, the hands of God. And you were held in them: yes, you were there: His people, held in His hands. The vision was glorious. I knew that I also was in His hands.

Then the vision changed and the hands started to move. There was no way you and I could be still in His hands. It was the Church of Jesus Christ being shaken by a God who loves them. It wasn't the devil that was shaking the Church, it was God. And how true it is that every so often we need to be shaken (Deuteronomy 32:11). Then the hands started to move in a way that I would describe as like a large cement mixer. The Church was being thrown all over the place, this way, that way. Every person was being moved.

When the hands stopped: when they stood still; every man, every woman, every person was in the place that they should have been. Not one member of the Church was out of place (John 10:27). Everyone was in the right place, with the right people, at the right time, with the right word. That is the perfect will of God for His people. And God will not settle until this happens in your and my life. For many have been sent out by man and not by God, many have taken the position because of employment and not because of calling. Many who say they are saved, are not. My friend: know the will of God for your life and walk in it.

As I am writing about the will of God for your life, can I ask you a very simple question? I have asked this question many times in my life, and within a grouping of people, the same answers will come from them. The question I would like to ask you is, "Do you know the will of God for your life?"

Very few will say, "I am doing what I do, because God has called me!" Most of the people will say the following... "Well, I hope, am right!" "Does anyone ever know the will of God for their life?" Comes the answer: "I'm praying about it?" How long does one need to pray about the will of God? Before long, you'll look into the mirror; and the face, no matter how much you creamed it, will no longer be youthful. What is even worse, there are those who say they're baptised in the Holy Spirit and not knowing they're in the will of God for their lives. How can that ever be?

Let me ask; "Were you baptised into a religion or a relationship?"

God wants you to know that He has not a generalised plan for you, but a specific plan. Why? Because you are special to Him. There is none like you: you are unique. No one else has your fingerprints, no one has your eyes; so why would you think you're average?

You need to know, that you know, that you're in the will of God over your life. For in that, you will see what no other sees; you will hear what no other hears; and you will run in a calling that no other can run in. That is God's desire for you.

Do you see the potential that is within you? What if you would only line up to His will over your life? God may not call you across the sea, but He might call you across the street. And you'll know it. And the results will be there to show, God called you. Never limit God to a church building, never limit Him to a mission field. It can be that; but not only that. Let me repeat this again: it's knowing that you're in the right place at the right time with the right Word to the right people. That is the call of God. And I believe that as each one of us fulfils this, we, the Church, will walk in revival.

As the vision ended with the hands moving, I was waiting in His presence. I knew that I knew: God was going to do something new my life. I knew God was not finished with me. Then I heard the cry of His people. I heard the cry of His Church. No earthly words would ever describe it.

And God said, "Have you heard this? Have you heard this cry?"

I said, "Yes, Lord."

And then God asked, "What will you do about this cry?"

Oh, reader; there's a place in God where pretence must be removed from us, or we cannot go any further. When God asked that question, my answer was, "Oh God, there is nothing I can do about it. Nothing!" And God said, "That is right. There is nothing you can do about it. But rise, stand on your feet, and go!"

This was around 4.30am in the morning in Germany, and still there was a group of young people on their knees next door praying for a move of God. One stood up and started to prophesy in German, it was a young man called Frank. I said, "Tell me Frank, can you share with me the prophecy?" He shared with me that God had heard the affliction of His people, He knew their sorrows, and He heard their cry. He has come down to deliver them. Then he told me, "God said that He would send you!"

You see, I was not into all this travelling to be seen, be spoilt, honoured; and, not forgetting the other side, having to share my bed with a big smelly dog, no heat in the bedroom, no door on the bedroom, eating food that an animal has just licked over, because the homeowner would otherwise have been offended; oh, I would tell you stories! Friend, ministry is not about glamour: it's about reaching souls.

Even you: God has come down to deliver you. To take you to a place where He is Lord and everything must bow under His feet.

CHAPTER 21

IT'S GOD'S LOVE OR NOTHING?

I can never look at the following Scriptures in John 16:27-28 and not be moved in my spirit, without seeing the love of Jesus.

> *'For the Father Himself loves you, because you have loved Me, and have believed that I came forth from God. I came forth from the Father and have come into the world. Again, I leave the world and go to the Father.'*

Now isn't that something? Jesus, being God, knowing all things, came to this earth for you and me. And an hour comes when He says, 'I will go back to the Father'. But do you think the disciples believed him? Somehow I believe the disciples thought he would always be there, so in Him saying He was leaving, the disciples became sorrowful.

Jesus has a special love for His own people, and this is shown in these Scriptures and those in John 13, where He takes a towel and a basin of water and knelt at men's feet... now isn't that LOVE! The One who left the glory of heaven kneels down at the feet of men.

Nothing in Scripture is by accident. He was willing to come to you. Now He's come to His hour where all things at this moment were to be finished. Jesus knelt and took the lowly task of the servant, the lowest servant in a house; and washed their feet.

Love is not selective, knows no colour or creed. Can you imagine him washing Peter's feet; knowing that He was going to deny him even with curses? And yet love washed Peter's feet. He washed Judas' feet... My friend, don't overlook what is happening here. He washed Judas' feet, the feet of the betrayer. He came to Thomas, the one who would not believe 'except I see the nail prints', and so on.... And guess what? These were his disciples that were being entrusted with the Gospel.

Love is the greatest power in the universe, Love never fails! Can you say that out loud: 'Love never fails!?' God is love and love is God. Calvary tells us that the greatest love that we can ever taste is the love of Jesus. His love is deeper; purer; not corrupt; it's His great love, the love He gave to His own... loving them to the end. He said, "You see what I have done for you?" If the Lord and Master would wash your feet, wash you the feet of others.

Jesus went to His Father as the custom was. And the Father would have spoken and said, "A new commandment I give to you... that you love one another. The Ten Commandments are for the world, the New Commandment is for the church. I wonder: have you broken that commandment? For Jesus said, if you keep this commandment, all men will know that you are my disciples.

It's not important to know whether people know us for being Baptist, Pentecostal, Presbyterian; it is important that they know we have Jesus' love. Jesus said our sins are buried in the deepest sea and will not be remembered anymore... (Micah 7:19). That is what love does.... it forgives and forgets. It does not say that we have to help each other, for we can help and not love. But you cannot love and then not help.

The first time I read this Scripture I thought, 'There is no way I can be your disciple... for I have always tried to be honest before God when I was a young Christian'. I told him "I cannot be your disciple." God said, "Why can you not be my disciple?" I replied to Him, "Because I don't like what I saw in the church". God said, "I don't like some of the things either, but I have not commanded you to like them, I have commanded you to love them."

His love will keep you where nothing else will. As Scripture says... *'Though I speak with the tongues of men and of angels, but have not love, I have become sounding brass or a clanging cymbal.'* 1 Corinthians 13:1

CHAPTER 22

DOES GOD STILL SPEAK?

I believe that when we meet in the Lord Jesus, something good will happen. We are not here by chance, we are here by divine appointment. God has a plan, a purpose for this hour and He knows who you are; He knows where you are; and He knows how you are; and in that knowledge He will speak to your heart.

God has a word for this hour: He is not dead; He's alive. God is not silence: He speaks, and there is so much He wants to show you and to give you. He will come to those who wait; He will speak to those who have an ear to hear; and enter the hearts of those who are open to Him. I pray that God will receive a hundredfold in the seed that He has planted within you. For He is worthy of such.

The days that we live in are exciting days. There is so much happening in this world and I've got good news to share. Every time I read my Bible, every new day that I arise, every time I pray, every time I come into the house of God, there is a stirring in my spirit; there is an urgency in my heart for the word of God that has been put in my heart. Every time God has told me to share this word, lives are changed; from the youngest to the oldest. The Church awakes and many, many people come to Jesus. Backsliders are restored, the Church is revived. Prayer becomes a new dimension; reality is in place; 'trivia-reality' is gone.

Take this in carefully. If you only hear John Hamilton, forget it. God wants you to hear His voice; and you will know it. And when God speaks to your heart something happens inside! Revelation of His love; revelation of Heaven; revelation of your need for Him. His word is infallible, impregnable, it cannot be broken, it cannot lie, all that God speaks He will do, all that God promises He will give; so if you're a believer, you're a favourite people and God has ordained this hour that you should come under His word.

Let us read the word of God in Luke 3:2 '...*the word of God came to John the son of Zacharias in the wilderness.*'

Let me ask you... "Do you believe that God can speak to you when you're in a wilderness? In fact let me make it clearer? Do you believe that God can speak to you in the middle of your wilderness?" When you're in that dry barren empty place where no water is, where no hope is, where no life is, God even can speak there!

Here we read that John was in the wilderness; and what a word that God gave to him! And if you're in a wilderness God can speak to you. You do not need to be in a great spiritual condition. You can be in a wilderness and as God spoke to John, He can speak to you. God is not bound, He can speak in all places, in all conditions, in all circumstances; after all is He not Lord of all, the Lord God Almighty!?

Isaiah (40:3) writes: '*The voice of one crying in the wilderness: 'Prepare the way of the* LORD; MAKE HIS PATHS STRAIGHT.*

83

Every valley shall be filled and every mountain and hill brought low; the crooked places shall be made straight and the rough ways smooth; and <u>all flesh</u> *shall see the salvation of God.'* (Luke 3:4-6)

Did you read that?... All flesh: not some; but <u>all flesh</u> shall see the salvation of God!

Isn't that something! Isn't that just wonderful, surely that in itself stirs up your heart? If you were not to read anything else in this book, surely that should have set your heart on fire! It should heal every backslider, it should bring you into a new place in your spiritual walk; for that day will come when the word of God will be fulfilled, because God cannot lie and that day is near.

One of my favourite hymns is...

Open our eyes Lord, we want to see Jesus,
To reach out and touch Him, and say that we love Him.
Open our ears Lord, and help us to listen.
Open our eyes Lord, we want to see Jesus.
(Author Robert Cull)

The Bible says, *'Nevertheless when one turns to the Lord, the veil is taken away. Now the Lord is the Spirit; and where the Spirit of the Lord is, there is liberty. But we all, with unveiled face, beholding as in a mirror the glory of the Lord, are being transformed into the same image from glory to glory, just as by the Spirit of the Lord.* 2 Corinthians 3:16-18

Each time I sing that, I ask the Father to take away my spiritual cataracts, take away the dumbness from my ears. Help us to reach out and touch You, Lord; for the King is coming.

CHAPTER 23

THE KING IS COMING

Are you aware that the King is coming? Do you know when he is coming? He is coming next Monday, yes, he is. You don't believe me? This is what I heard as a little boy in school in Scotland when the teacher said, "The King is coming and he is coming next Monday!" But she was not speaking about the King of kings she was speaking about the King of England.

He was coming to Scotland and our hearts were full of joy. The teacher then announced, "We will forget your school lessons for today. Come and sit around my desk." And for one hour she told us about the King of England, about his Majesty, about his palace, about his wealth and all his power. And the hearts of us all were just so thrilled and she said, "When he comes, boys and girls, he will come in a golden carriage driven by six white horses."

Now I know many of you reading this book have likely never been given the chance to see the King of England, but can you imagine it? This was happening when I was a little boy with so much depression, so much poverty, people were very poor but when the news came… The King is Coming!… it lifted the depression, we actually forgot we were poor, we all began to sing, 'The King is

Coming, The King is Coming'. The teacher then said, "Before he comes, we must get ready, we must clean the place up"; and everywhere in Scotland the people were scrubbing, washing, cleaning to get ready for the King. Oh, I cannot even express here the excitement! And no matter where you went, people were shining things, and if you stood long enough, they would be shining you if you had been there. But on the Sunday night before the day of his arrival, I have to say... I will never forget that Sunday night.

That night, all the mothers in Scotland scrubbed their children. There was six of us and with no bathroom, no shower room, no privacy, just a great big metal tub in the middle of the living room floor and one was just stripped and told... "into the tub!" You see, you've got to be clean for the King to come! My mother scrubbed all six of us until each one was tingling and all of us were sparkling clean. Then off to bed, the six of us sleeping in the one bed, three at the top and three at the bottom. You went in alive and came out dead, somebody's feet, arms or legs lying over the top of you. That night it was difficult to sleep with the excitement but at some point we all drifted over.

Even though it was Monday, in the morning each one of us was dressed in our best Sunday clothes; after all... the King is coming!

From early dawn, hundreds and hundreds of people had already gathered, everyone was waiting on the arrival of the King. The people were singing and laughing, I never had witnessed such a good time and then just one hour before the King arrives, the rain comes down, drenching rain, and all the ladies who had spent a fortune getting perms in their hair were now looking like wet mop heads and none of them complained because they wanted to see the King. Then in the distance, a shout went up, "THE KING IS HERE!" Oh, I can see and feel the excitement from that day! I saw the white horses, I saw the golden carriage, but I didn't see the King... do you know why? A great big policeman took a step and stood right in front of me. And I couldn't see the King. After all what I went through... getting scrubbed, waiting for hours on the street and in the rain, I did not see the one I had dressed for, the King. All I saw was his hand waving. From that moment on, I told everyone I had seen the King's hand, and he waved at me. You know how people can pour cold water on your celebration, even if it is only half-true? When I told others of seeing the King's hand, they told me they had seen the King's face. I would respond, "Where is his power? It is not in his face, it is in his hand." And for days, weeks and months, everyone was speaking about the King.

Where I was raised was not a very popular place, the men were rough and tough, they never spoke nice, but when they saw the King you know what they said? They said, "Wasn't the King lovely, wasn't the King beautiful." They never said such words before, they never even told their wives they were beautiful but they said "The King is beautiful!" You see my friend, when you see the King, the effects can change your language, change your heart. The King only passed through and we never saw him again. But in coming he left an impact.

But I have better news than that for you! I have greater news than that! The King of kings is coming! I cannot say, "He is coming next Monday," but I can tell you, He is coming soon! Every time I read my Bible I know it, every time I pray I feel it, the King is coming and this King is not going to pass by, He will not go away, He is coming for His Church, His people, to take us to glory. He said, *'Let not your heart be troubled; you believe in God, believe also in Me. In My Father's house are many mansions, if it were not so, I would have told you, I will come again and receive you to Myself; that where I am, there you may be also. And where I go you know, and the way you know.'* John 14:1-4

Oh, am looking forward to that day when the King of kings comes! I will go with Him, because I have got royal blood in me: the blood of Jesus.

Jesus said, *'I am the Way, the Truth and the life. No one comes to the Father except through Me.'* John 14:6 Do you realise there is no other way? There is only one way! And Jesus is the way to heaven... now isn't that good news! Get ready! Get ready! Jesus is coming again: not to die on a cross, not to be mocked or crucified by men; but He's coming as a King of kings and Lord of lords. What a day that will be, when He comes for His own when King Jesus breaks through the clouds and the shout has gone up in Heaven, *'Behold, I come quickly!'* (Revelation 20:12)! And the Church will respond... *'Even so, come Lord Jesus!'* (Revelation 20:20). Will that be your response?

Do you know: every time you hear the gospel, every time you pray, every time God touches your heart, every time God cleanses you, it is to bring you into that place where you are ready for that hour. He wants you to be ready. That was the word that John the Baptist received in the wilderness from God... *'Prepare ye the way of the Lord!'*

John's central message was... Jesus the Messiah is coming! (John 1). Everywhere he went this is what he preached... 'Behold the

Lamb of God", "Behold! The Lamb of God is coming" If you're a believer, then you know that the hour John preached about came to pass. Men did not believe it, some even laughed, closed their hearts to it and yet the hour came! For God cannot break His word. He was born in a stable for there was no room in the inn. He came to His own and they did not receive Him. When He entered the ministry at age 30 years of age, everywhere He went He set people free, healed people, because He was sent from the Father. You need to know that the Holy Spirit is working on you. He is convicting you because He wants you to be ready for that hour. The word that John got was a mighty word; but the word that Jesus gave about the last hour, the word you are reading now, is a mightier word.

Every time you read your newspaper... every time you watch the news... every time you hear of how evil this world is becoming... He is coming, my friend, Jesus is coming!

Listen, we are not living in the last days. We are living in the last hour! Time is running out and the voice of the trumpet is sounding! Jesus is coming and a declaration has gone forth... *'Prepare ye the way of the Lord!'* This is what God is asking you to do: Prepare the way for His coming! What we must do is to make the path of the Lord straight. If the path of the Lord is not straight in your heart, you need to ask God to make it straight. Why? Because when God gives this word, it means the church is corrupt, unclean, vile; when all the time it should be the opposite.

People don't know which way to go because one church says, 'go this way', another church says, 'go that way' and the both churches do not speak to each other. Oh my, my, do you think Heaven will have non-speakers within its gates, those who despise each other, those who condemn each other... we need to prepare the way my friends. We need to be a manifestation of God's love, instead condemning a brother/sister we should be reaching down and lifting them... that is how we straighten the road of our hearts by adjusting the dial on our mindsets to God and not carnal flesh.

This is our part: to give ourselves to God, to be His voice, to make His path straight again. Then God promises that every valley shall be filled! If you've been in a valley, this is your way out of the place where you cannot praise God, the valley of depression, the valley where you cannot see a way out. It's a very lonely place, a dark place, can I even dare to say... an ugly place. But if you become His voice, then every valley will be filled. Oh my, you may have fallen into the valley; but when you start being His voice, the water of the Holy Spirit will come. For you or me, who cannot get out of the valley, the Holy Spirit will raise Himself and lift you and me out as we prepare the way of the Lord.

You don't need to be in the valley anymore, you just need to know that God wants to raise you out of the valley. You were never redeemed for the valley; you were redeemed for the heavenlies. Scripture says, 'But those who wait on the Lord shall renew their strength. They shall mount up with wings like eagles, they shall run and not be weary, they shall walk and not faint.' (Isaiah 40:31)

Where does the eagle have dominion? It makes its domain in the heavenlies and that is what God wants for His people. He does not want you in a valley; He wants you in heavenly places. He wants you to be above and not underneath. He wants you to be more than conquerors and not conquered. For He paid the price in full to redeem you in cleansing you, in bringing you back into fellowship with the Father, and "the Father's will is for you to be where I am" (Jesus said).

David ran into a valley: not to stay in it, but to fight the giant called Goliath who dominated the valley (1 Samuel 17). In other words, David ran through the valley, because he knew it was not God's will for him to stay in the valley. Far too many Christians are in the valley, allowing the valley to swamp their lives, and that is not a testimony to the saving power of Jesus. Why not let God put a new song in your mouth? Then the joy of the Lord can be your strength, and you can stand and not fall because He can fill your valley.

I thanked God that He filled that valley for me. Yes, there have been times when I have been tempted to stay in a valley: but when you understand the price, the suffering the pain of what Jesus went through to get us out of the valleys; can I ask... why are we still within it? I ask you to start stepping out in the promises of God, for they cannot fail. Learn to look up rather than looking down; look up, because your redemption draws nigh! My Saviour is getting ready to come again. As you look up and live in the state of readiness, your prayer life will not be poor, your witness will not be dull, you will be on fire for God. You will be ablaze with the Spirit. The Word tells me that this message purifies the Church.

There is such richness in this Word for you, for He promises that He will bring the mountains low. How is that going to happen? The waters of the Spirit will raise you and what would have looked enormous one time in your life: sin, sickness, trouble etc.; He will make a way where there is no way! (Isaiah 43:19)

I went into itinerary ministry and have travelled many years, spoken in thousands of churches, many, many countries and again, again and again I must tell you: the church is unclean, the church is divided, the church is weak, the church is crooked, the church is so fearful of what other churches will think. I don't care if you believe that or not, I have seen it with my own eyes and I have wept over the state of the church.

God wants to make the crooked straight: He wants you and me to be straight. Will you search your heart regarding this word? Do not turn to the right or the left (Joshua 1:7) but look into your own heart now. Are you being straight before God? Is there any shade of crookedness in your life? Can you say: 'Everything I do and say can come under the searchlight of the Holy Spirit'? 'I have nothing to hide, nothing to fear, God knows my heart, I am not crooked.'

God wants you to walk before men without fear and that comes when we walk straight before God. What do people see in you? Are you a living testimony of the saving power of our Lord Jesus Christ? This generation of Christians will be responsible for this generation of sinners. We have been sent as salt of the earth and light in a dark world (Matthew 5:13-14). Make yourself ready before the Lord before the cry comes… The King is here!

If I had a white sheet and in the corner was a small black spot, what would your attention be drawn to? Everyone I ask this question will answer… the black spot!

The Word of God tells me that the prayer of Jesus, the desire of Jesus, is to present you without spot or blemish (Ephesians 5:27). Can you just for a moment take that in? Our Lord and

Saviour Jesus Christ wants to present you to His Father without spot or blemish. He wants to say to His Father, while pointing to you and me... 'My bride, pure, holy and clean.' Is He not worthy of that honour: that you and I will be clean for that day of presentation to the Father? Even now He is interceding for you and me. Listen, He's not praying that you might be happy but that you might be holy.

The church has tried so hard to get people happy and now we are reaping a generation of emotional believers, driven by the flesh (weakness, backsliding, coldness), and not by the Spirit who is Holy. When we become a holy nation, a royal priesthood (1 Peter 2:9), then and only then will we, the church, be a power to be reckoned with for this generation.

Every unforgiven sin, every sin that is not cleansed: Christ weeps over it, and if you have sin in the camp, He weeps over your sin. You're his child and He wants to bring you to the Father. In that hour He wants to say: My bride, My Church, redeemed, cleansed and made clean by my blood.

We the Church have been redeemed: not for a moment, but for every day of our lives. If the Church will walk in this way, if the Church will have this testimony, then the crooked will be made straight, the rough made smooth, the mountains and the hills be brought low, valleys filled; and there will be a voice in the wilderness declaring, *'Prepare the way of the Lord!'* When this happens, the world that is around you will see the salvation of the Lord through you. Do you want the world around you to see the salvation of the Lord? The key is within your hand, the answer is within your heart... call upon the Name of the Lord and be saved. I want that day to come, I want that hour to break that when church gathers people who will not laugh nor poke fun; for they will see the salvation of the Lord.

It's time for you to be real! Time for you to be honest! It's time to be right with God!

If Jesus was to come now, are you ready? Or will you be ashamed of His coming? What do you need to put right before He comes? Do you need to be washed from criticism, pornography, unforgiveness, resentment, crookedness, deceptiveness? You know what is in your heart?

This is not my opinion, not just another word. This is a word from heaven to the church tonight. Get ready, church; get ready by putting away the childish things, putting away the unclean things, putting away the foolish things. Bring everything under the Blood of the Lamb, Jesus Christ, and be clean, and be holy, and be ready, because the King is coming, yes, the King is coming... are you ready?

And when you're ready... you will begin to live in the power of Christ, you will walk in a new dimension, heaven will be near you, your heart is wider, your love is greater, no man can come against you there, you're more than conquerors, life is never dull, every day brings a newness in Christ, He makes heaven real and the things of this world will have no attraction; because heaven becomes your home, your destination, your assignment: eternity with the Master.

CHAPTER 24

GOD IS MORE THAN A SUNDAY?

I want to you share with you a story that I love. It's about a little girl whose parents were missionaries. One day the young girl asked her mother, "Where were you born?" Her mother answered, "I was born in England." Then the girl asked, "Where was daddy born?" Mother answered, "He was born in Scotland." Then she asked, "Where was I born?" "You were born here in India." Mother answered. The little girl looked at her mother and said, "You were born in England; Daddy in Scotland; and I was born here in India. Oh Mama, am so happy that God brought us together!"

I am so happy that God has brought us together for this hour. When we come into the presence of God, there is a stillness in His presence that brings healing, sets captives free, transforms our lives; and His name is Jesus.

God brings people together for one purpose that He would speak into our hearts, and His Word *will be a lamp to your feet and a light to your path* (Psalm 119:105).

'*When Jesus came into the region of Caesarea Philippi, He asked His disciples, saying, "Who do men say that I, the Son of Man, am?" So they said, "Some say* John the Baptist, *some* Elijah, *and others* Jeremiah *or one of the prophets." He said to them, "But who do you say that I am?" Simon Peter answered and said, "You are the Christ, the Son of the living God." Jesus answered and said to him, "Blessed are you, Simon Bar-Jonah, for flesh and blood has not revealed this to you, but My Father who is in heaven. And I also say to you that you are Peter, and on this rock I will build My church, and the gates of Hades shall not prevail against it. And I will give you the keys of the kingdom of heaven, and whatever you bind on earth will be bound in heaven, and whatever you loose on earth will be loosed in heaven.'* Matthew 16:13-19

I think this must be one of the saddest verses in the Bible, when we read Jesus saying, "Who do people say I am?" Jesus is the *gift* that God gave to the world. He was willing to leave the glory of Heaven where angels worshipped Him and where His Father loved Him. Because Jesus loved you so much and He wanted you to know the Father, there was only one way. He must leave the glory of Heaven and come to this earth as the Saviour of this world. Jesus knew all that was before Him! He knew that men would not believe Him. He knew that men would despise and reject Him. He knew that men would spit upon Him. He knew He would be crucified. Still He came – why? Because He loves you!

God's love is colour-blind, undying, unconditional love. His love never fails because He Himself is Love! (1 John 4:8)

For just over three years after the Jordan baptism He would minister to the multitude, healing the sick, setting the captive free. People would travel for miles to hear and see Him. There were no posters, no radios, no TV's; and yet how did they hear about our Saviour? When people went and told others that Jesus was in town, people left everything to come! And the testimony was... *'no man spoke like this man'* (John 7:46). His Word was with power and authority. He did not speak like the Scribes and the Pharisees. When He spoke, demons came out, the sick were healed and lives were changed. Yet, He asked the disciples... "Who do they say that I am?" They answered, "Some say you're John the Baptist; some say you're Elijah." The devil was trying to rob Jesus of His true name. The devil knew that God had exalted Jesus by giving Him a name above every name, that at the name of Jesus every knee shall bow, every tongue confess that Jesus Christ is Lord, the Anointed of the Father, the Son of the Living God. This is the testimony of every believer: that no man comes to the Father except through Him.

Jesus then asked His disciples one more question. Are you ready to hear what that question is? He asked them... *"Who do you say I am?"* Peter answered, *"You are the Christ, the Son of the Living God!"* Jesus responded, *"Blessed are you, Simon Bar-Jonah, for flesh and blood has not revealed this to you, but My Father who is in heaven."* God's desire in sending His Son to be the Saviour of the world was that we might be reconciled onto Him. That we might know Him? Not just know about Him. To know Him is more than information, it is revelation of the Holy Spirit. Can you say, "Once I was blind but now, I see." This one thing I know, yes one thing I know... I was blind and now I see! When you know Jesus, you will walk in light.

I want to ask you do you know Him? Do you know He is the Christ, the anointed of the Father, the only answer to every need? Do you know Him at that level?

I want to tell you that He is more than knowledge, He is Lord so that He can have your life and live in His fulness. The apostle Paul who wrote most of the New Testament still cried out... *'That I might know Him and the power of His resurrection...'* Philippians 3:10. You will never stop knowing Him, this is why He gives us eternity, for as eternity is unending, so in always getting to know our God. How exciting is that!

You need to understand that an associate may know you, but a friend will know you greater. But then your child will know you in a way your friend does not, and yet your partner will know you in a way that others do not know because they have lived with you and have came through circumstances with you.

In Scotland there is a saying... 'Love is blind but marriage is an eye-opening!'

We never get to know people truly just by visiting. You'll hear, "Hello, how are you?" Answer, "Praise God, I'm doing well!" But when you live with them, you'll see every spot, you'll see every blemish, you'll see everything that is not so good; but that is what it means to live with someone. There is no hiding, there is no covering, and this is where God wants us to be in the relationship with Him. Not that we just come in a crisis, not just to come for gifts, not just to come as a mighty preacher, but to know Him and to live in His presence. God has so much to give you and yet if we do not know Him, then part of you will remain empty.

To know Him we need time with Him, and that time will never be wasted in learning more about Him and yet you'll also learn about the real you. You see, He will show you the falseness of our walk in front of people, and point us to the reality of our walk in front of Him. Oh, how we have been programmed just to hear good things… "Oh, you're a wonderful person," and truly, do we know the real us? We know the murmuring within our hearts of failure in jealousy, pride and rebellion. But God will not condemn, He will be reaching in to swap what you have to receive who He is, the God of Love. Will you swap what is holding you back from walking in the fulness of God? He loves to make the weak strong; He delights to lift up the fallen, as you say to Him, "I want to know you!"

When you swap your life for His fulness, Scripture says, *'People who know their God shall be strong, and carry out great exploits'* (Daniel 11.32) for Him. Don't you want to do exploits for the Master?

Every weakness in your life is there because of you not really knowing Him! Oh, but you say I do know Him? But I ask, "At what level?" Is it that of an associate? For if it is, we need to put that right. He never died for us to be a pen-pal, He died that He could be all He needs to be within us.

No longer should your desire, be to stand at the shoreline and dip your little toe in. You need to jump right into Him, no fear, only love for Him. And as we jump into God, the generation around us who do not know Him will get to know Him through the God who has transformed you into His image, bringing glory to the Father and causing hell to tremble.

I just want to add one more point… I find it strange that the demons of hell know Jesus better than God's people. The demons said, *'What have we to do with You, Jesus, You Son of God? Have you come here to torment us before the time?'* Matthew 8:29.

Wouldn't that be something if that were the testimony of God's people? Hell coming against you! When temptation is knocking at your door, when the way is hard, the battle is bloody as a storm comes against you and the only way you can answer your door is to say: 'He is my Lord and I will go through the storm, for He is with me and will never leave me.' Out of my weakness I shall be made strong!

If you are reading this and you're ashamed of your weakness, ashamed of the poor testimony... (Oh, am not talking about the one on Sunday morning, I am talking about the one late at night, when no-one is watching, in the secret, in the darkness of the shadow that keeps you in defeat, to the point some days you can't even lift up your head...) can I ask... "Why? Has God ever lied?" For Scripture says, *'In my presence there is fulness of joy.'* (Psalms 16:11. It does not say, 'fulness of laughter', but 'fulness of joy!'

Joy is not dependent on our circumstances: that's happiness. Joy is that of the Lord, like Paul when in prison (Acts 16), he sang. He did not sing because it was the right thing to do, he sang because of the Spirit of joy within him, *knowing that with God all things are possible and even though He would slay me, yet would I trust Him.* (Job 13:15)

Can you say, "I want to know Him?" Tomorrow and every day after, can you rise with those words in your mouth... "I want to know Him!" My, my, how our lives would differ!

What did he say?

> He lifted me from all my sin and shame,
> He lifted me all glory to His name,
> He lifted me I'll never be the same,
> Hallelujah Jesus lifted me.

Father, I thank you for this hour and for all you have said and done in our hearts already. Thank you for the moving of Your Holy Spirit, how we need You to move again and again. I pray with all of my heart that You would help us to not just be hearers only but that we would also become doers of Your Word; that this generation would know the God who saves, heals and delivers His people.

CHAPTER 25

HE SENT THEM OUT IN TWO'S

John was a man full of surprises, and on one of our ministry trips to Germany we were boarding in England and of course, because I had booked from Belfast and he was booked from Leeds, we had not been allocated to sit beside each other, he says to me… "Hold off till everyone gets on board, Maurice, and then we will go on." Obediently, I waited. Then he went on and I was following him and he stopped with the stewardess and said, "This is my son and we need to sit beside each other. Can you organise this?" Now if you had known John: he would have put a face on that you would give him your last Rolo sweet without hesitation. But there was no response from all the people sitting now; and then he does it… He turns to the whole airplane passengers himself, puts his sad face on and says, "Would anyone swap one of your seats so that my son and I can sit beside each other?" About six people rose from across the plane all offering us their seats. Now is that not the love of a father? It was never about arriving; it was about how we would arrive… he would spend that time sharing with me.

Arriving at a German Church where Adolf Hitler married his officers during the time of the war, we were ushered up the stairs into the Vestry and told, "Don't touch anything. I'll be back in

30 minutes to bring you into the main hall for the ministry time." Telling John, "Don't touch anything" was like telling a child "don't lick the ice cream" that is within their reach. Around this lovely vestry hung a number of robes, and, looking at them, I knew they were extremely expensive. And here was John, saying "Let's try them on!" "What, we've just been told not to even touch them?" "Do you not remember, he said they have been sanctified"; and he made it very clear not to touch the robes. My words were falling on deaf ears, and before I knew it, there was John stretching himself the best he could to unhook the coat hanger that the robe was on, but he couldn't reach it. He's telling me to come over here and lift this down, and all I was thinking about was this minister coming back and us two clowns in the middle of a dress rehearsal with sanctified robes!

It was not stopping John, neither was his shortness of height. Within seconds he had pulled a chair over and, standing up on it, he reached over and lifted the robe down. Then forgetting about his height (or did he?), he ended up trailing the robe across the carpet as it was that long. Next thing he says, "Right, help me get this on?" Oh, what do you do in such a case, because part of me was laughing at like a six-foot robe in length and here was a man not more than five feet tall wanting it on? He wore the robe and screwed up his face, I still have that photo of him… unreal.

I would like to tell you that it ended there but no, he would not stop harassing me until he got the robe on me and of course nothing would do except him getting on his knees and asking me to bless him… "I bless thee, holy father!!!" Then we heard the steps, he runs over and sits down on the chair, I have returned the robes to the hangers, the minister walks in and examines the room, almost as if he was not able to trust us. Then he said the words: "Are you ready? Let's go." John winked at me and off we went… we had survived another moment of his sense of humour. It's ok to not always be serious and to have fun!

Another time John and I had just arrived from a two-three-hour flight, been collected at the airport and taken to a house where we would be staying for the weekend. Came teatime, and we were called to the table to eat. After the house owner saying grace, we started to eat. I had noticed John was not eating the meat, so with me being a quick eater, I was nearly finished and John kept making faces at me and towards his plate. Of course, I'm near full, but I am accepting that he's wanting to know if I wanted his meat. But in my nodding, 'No', John asks the host, can he leave it. The host went into a fit: "What is wrong with the food?" John trying to explain there was nothing wrong with the food. John just told him, it's ok he would eat it. But the problem was he was finding it hard to swallow (this was the start of his throat problems). So what did John do… he nodded at me and every time the host would not be looking, he shot a piece of the food over to my plate, and together we finished his dinner. Sometimes to stop people being offended and closing their heart, we need to see a way around the obstacle. After all we don't know what they had been going through… and love covers a mistake.

John had a wild sense of humour; but more than that, he had the love of God.

On his last trip to me, I had collected him at the airport. He had aged and knew he was not well, but he tried his best not to show it. As we got into the car he said to me, how long do we have before the meeting starts? I told him, several hours. He said, "Do you know where Whiteabbey is?" "Yes!" I said. And he asked, "Can we go there!" Off we went, with me not even knowing why I was going. When we got to the edge of Whiteabbey I asked was there any specific place he wanted to go to? He handed me an address, but he had not taken it down right. Then he remembered that a man had written to him asking for ministry... here was John, literally dying; and this man was not aware he was out searching for him. That day he and I spent driving up and down nearly every road around Whiteabbey looking for something that would spark his memory in the letter which the man had written. That day we left Whiteabbey, not finding the man; but for me an understanding of leaving the 99 for the one.

On the way back to Ballymena, we stopped to get some soup and as we were waiting, here starts John with one of his stories...

"I know you have been to India, Maurice, but did I ever tell you about my time in India?" "No!" I answered, and off he went...

I was invited to India to minister and I still remember clearly sitting in an old large hut. The ladies were making the lunch and I was chatting to the pastors waiting for the lunch. We were having soup and the ladies were making it in a very large saucepan, about two feet deep and same in width. The pan was set on top of several bricks with the fire in the middle and it did smell good. But as I was sitting talking away to the pastors, my eye caught a young boy going over to the pan. I thought he was going to try and lift a spoonful of soup but not so, it was worse than that. He looked around and saw no one looking, dropped his shorts a little and peed into the saucepan. Maurice, it wasn't just a wee pee, it was a long pee and I knew that I knew, this was going to be my soup.

Of course Maurice, you know, when they set the food in front of you (and for those poor people who have sacrificed so much to make the food), it is totally wrong not to eat it... well I ate the soup with a grin on my face swallowing it as quick as I could. To be honest with you... I was swallowing it that quick, I never tasted it! Just then, the lady in our restaurant in Ballymena served us their soup... for me it now had taken on a whole new meaning!

CHAPTER 26

A GOD STANDARD...

At times we can all be surrounded by voices of darkness, especially when we are in a valley; and how difficult it is to be joyful in that moment. There were times when John Hamilton was surrounded by darkness and in valleys, especially when the doctor would have given him bad news, voices whispering to him that he would never get out of the valley. I remember collecting him from the airport and he would look into my eyes with those beady eyes of his, and ask, "Well, Maurice; is today's testimony honouring the God you serve?" He had a way of just pushing out of the way anything that one thought was important and just coming in with what I would call a 'God standard'.

That night on the way to the meeting, he was spitting blood: he had been diagnosed with cancer of the throat. I had known him for about 15 years at this point and before we left, he said to me... "You know Maurice, it's not what you go through; it's how you go through it!" I hope you, the reader, are taking this in?

He shared with me how ill he was, that in many ways he should not have been over in Northern Ireland, but his love for his spiritual son brought him. He shared about the day the doctor had told about the cancer and when he went home… oh, my friend, listen to this, for I know this was not just a moment in his life, this was his lifestyle. He left his wife in the living room and he went down to the place where he prayed. With every part of his being, he said, "devil, if this is all you have, if this is where you think is my lowest of the low in this valley of cancer, I want to let you hear something…". He opened his lungs and sang with every part of his being hands lifted up.

> Father, Son, and Holy Spirit
> Father, Son, and Holy Spirit
> Father, Son, and Holy Spirit
> With all my heart I worship only You.

He drew himself into God's presence. Then, in telling me all of this, he would say… "Maurice, what are you going through?" Oh, my heart wrenched in pain! Here was my spiritual dad telling me he was dying, yet he was asking me… what standard was I setting for what I was going through? My friend, what standard are we setting for others? Let the joy of the LORD be your strength.

John was deteriorating and now spending most of the time in bed. I decided to ring just to hear how he was. Zillah answered the phone and began to tell me; then in the background I heard a now weakened voice ask, "Who is it, Zillah?" She answered, "It's Maurice". "Give me the phone" John said.

I asked him, "How are you?" He replied, "I'm fine son, more importantly how are you?" Tears welled up in me. Here was this man I had now known for many years and again he blows me out of the box thinking; asking me how I was while as the time he was in his last moments upon the earth. It didn't matter what I was going through that day, who had died (if anyone), what I lost, who had fallen out with whom, etc., etc. For the first time I was alright because I had to be; because of a spiritual dad who not just confessed he was alright but lived in a place in God, where the Master had everything in control.

That day when the phone went down, I knew I would never speak to him again upon the earth. A couple of days later the call came, "John has passed away."

I am one of those people who suffer delayed shock. Next few hours I thought about him but then out of nowhere came a pain... my spiritual father had died. Oh, I cried like a child, the pain was enormous.

When my wife Maureen and I went to England for his celebration of his life, the wee (I'll use his word) Methodist Hall was packed to it was overflowing. People and pastors from across the world were in attendance. Several got up to pay their tribute, men in their eighties sang the old hymns and choruses that John loved. It was such a wonderful day. Many from Germany and across Europe came the distance. It was a day I'll never forget, and a man I'll forever love.

I'll leave you with one of the many visions God had given to him...

A VISION

While John was in America ministering, he was out for a walk through the countryside and had entered a large field to stroll along it. As he was walking he heard hundreds of horses running from behind. The noise was becoming louder and louder, so loud that he realised he was about to be run over. He grasped his head in his hands and turned to face the noise expecting to see a large herd of horses, likely about to run over him: but nothing was there. In that split second, he saw a vision of an extremely large thing that looked like cement mixer. But the outer part of the barrel was God's hands, and inside His hands were His people. As God moved His hands, the people were falling over each other, turning upside down etc., like sand in the mixer. After a moment His hands stopped moving and everything settled.

John asked God what was the meaning of that? God said, "My prodigals are coming home!" You see, people have made their own decisions of where to be and who to be, and then they wondered why things never worked out. But God was saying that He was going to shake the Church, bringing some of the pastors into the pews, because He never called them to pastor; and also taking some in the pews into ministry offices. As they positioned themselves in God in the right place, they were able to run like never before… the hoofs of the prodigals are returning!

INSPIRED TO WRITE A BOOK?

Contact
Maurice Wylie Media
Inspirational Christian Publisher

Based in Northern Ireland and distributing across the world.

www.MauriceWylieMedia.com